The Black Church in the Post–Civil Rights Era

Anthony B. Pinn

ORBIS BOOKS

Maryknoll, New York 10545

Copyright © 2002 by Anthony B. Pinn

Published by Orbis Books, Maryknoll, NY 10545-0308.

Manufactured in the United States of America
Manuscript editing and typesetting by Joan Weber Laflamme

Every effort has been made to ensure that the URLs in this book are accurate and up to date. However, with the rapid changes that occur in the World Wide Web, it is inevitable that some pages or other resources will have been discontinued or moved, and some content modified or reorganized. The publisher recommends that readers who cannot find the sources or information they seek with the URLs in this book use one of the numerous search engines available on the Internet.

Unless otherwise noted, scripure quotations are from the *King James Bible*.

Library of Congress Catloguing-in-Publication Data

Pinn, Anthony B.
   The Black church in the post–civil rights era / Anthony B. Pinn.
     p. cm.
   Includes bibliographical references.
   ISBN 1–57075–423–3 (pbk.)
    1. African American churches—History. 2. African Americans—Religion. I. Title

BR563.N4 P49 2002
280'.089'96073—dc21

2001052078

Dedicated to my wife, Cheryl Johnson,
and
the Ancestors

Contents

PART I
HISTORICAL AND THEOLOGICAL BACKGROUND

PART II
THEMES IN CONTEMPORARY PRAXIS

Acknowledgments

The conceptualizing and completion of this project have been a challenge. And although I alone am responsible for flaws in its content, I share credit for its better elements with many people. I cannot possibly name them all here, but I must mention a few. I begin with Robert Ellsberg and the staff of Orbis Books for their encouraging support of this project. I would like to offer my heartfelt thanks to: Rev. Anne H. Pinn, Darrell Drumwright, Jacqueline Trussell, Richard Killmer, Cheryl Kirk-Duggan, Evelyn Parker, and Preston Williams for assistance in securing materials and for providing their rich insights. I am grateful to Stephen Angell for reading several drafts of this project and making important suggestions for its improvement. Macalester College provided research and travel funds and a sabbatical during which I completed most of this project. The members of my Department worked doubly hard so that I could carve out space for my sabbatical work. Thank you. Several good friends in Minnesota helped me keep this project (and all the others) in perspective: thank you Richard Ammons, Robbie Seals (Got it right!), and Ahmed Samatar. I am particularly grateful to my close friend Ramón Rentas who spent much of his free time reading an earlier version of this manuscript and offering suggestions for improvement. Two friends from New York, Benjamin Valentin and Elieser Valentin, provided support, encouragement, and plenty of good jokes.

As always, I would like to thank my family for its support. I am grateful to my wife, Cheryl Johnson, to whom this volume is dedicated, for her love, support, good humor, and confidence in me. Finally, I am humbled by my ancestors who forged the Black Church and other resources for survival and social transformation.

Note on Terminology

Based on current literature, readers will probably approach this text with an understanding of "African American" as the commonly used term for the community under discussion here. This is typically true. However, for this exploration of the Black Church I use the adjective "black" as opposed to *African* American. Because this church developed in response to racial tensions and prejudices, I believe using the terms "black" and "white" keeps this racial conflict in the forefront of the discussion better than the terms "African American" and "European American." Related to this, before emancipation I refer typically to enslaved black Americans as Africans (and white Americans as Europeans) to denote the center of their history. After emancipation it is more common for me to use the following phrases: "those of African descent" or "black Americans," and "white Americans."

Furthermore, I use the phrase "Black Church" to denote the collective reality of black Christianity across denominational lines. My use of the phrase "black churches" more typically relates to local churches within a particular denomination. Context, however, makes the usage apparent.

Introduction

New York City usually conjures visions of night life and cultural revolution—the home of Broadway theater, the Cotton Club, and the Harlem Renaissance with its visionary figures such as Duke Ellington and Langston Hughes. It is also the place where Malcolm X and Marcus Garvey brought to the attention of the world the plight of black Americans through fiery forms of black nationalism framed by religious sensibilities. These events and persons express the richness of Manhattan, but Manhattan is not the only borough in New York of vital importance in black American history. Black Americans have resided in Brooklyn since the seventeenth century.[1] Brooklyn was home to the musician Hubey Blake, whose playing blended the "secular" and "sacred" elements of black American musical expression. And who can ignore the thriving art scene made famous by figures such as Spike Lee? Besides these forms of cultural vibrancy, Brooklyn is known for its many churches.

One of these churches is Washington Temple Church of God in Christ. On any given Sunday members of the church gather, participate in the singing of songs, the saying of prayers, and the reading of scripture and announcements, all in anticipation of the service's main element—the sermon. Before the sermon the morning hymn is sung, offerings taken, and visitors welcomed. The final transition to the preached word takes place as the worship leader introduces Reverend Madison, the pastor, who provides his testimony—outlining the various blessings given him by God—as members of the congregation have done earlier. The pastor approaches the pulpit and reminds the congregation of the scriptural lesson for the day, and the sermon begins with remarks on the need for obedience to God and the negative consequences of disobeying God's word. The pastor speaks of Jonah and the need to obey God that his adventure demonstrates—swallowed by a whale as he seeks to disregard God's call to preach the gospel to a group Jonah dislikes. There is a link, the preacher continues, between this episode and the church's call to evangelize, because all people stand in need of God's love. With all the energy the pastor can muster, he proclaims God's love for humanity and the responsibility of humans to embrace God and God's will through acceptance of Jesus Christ. Once this relationship with God through Christ is established, Reverend Madison continues by saying the power of God can be used in daily living. In response to the pastor's message, members of the congregation proclaim their support through a process of "call and response," by which the pastor's words are greeted with "Preach!," "Amen!," and "Praise the Lord!"

Each Sunday a similar scene of worship can be found in thousands of black churches across the country. Although only lasting a few hours, it is a central element of what defines the black Christian experience as housed in black churches. Scholars of black American religious history such as Carter Woodson, Benjamin Mays, and C. Eric Lincoln have argued the importance of the Black Church in the development of black communities and their civil rights, some going as far as to label it the lifeblood of the collective community.[2] According to the U.S. Census Bureau, there were approximately 34 million black Americans in the United States in 1998. Of this number, roughly 94 percent of those polled indicated they had prayed to God within the week. Black Americans were more than twice as likely as whites to have read the Bible during a given week. Questions related to actual church involvement and concrete Christian commitment were even more revealing. In 1999, roughly 49 percent of black Americans (roughly 27 million) labeled themselves "spiritual." Sixty-one percent of black Americans (roughly 20 million) called themselves "committed born-again Christians." Of these born-again, church-going black Americans the majority are located in seven denominations—three Methodist churches, three Baptist conventions, and one Pentecostal church.[3]

These major denominations and smaller black denominations together constitute the Black Church. This does not mean that these various denominations are homogeneous. Nonetheless, this term—the Black Church—speaks to the vibrancy of a shared tradition of Christian commitment that has helped shape the collective black community. It is true that not all black Christians make black churches their spiritual home. The substantial numbers in the Roman Catholic Church, for example, attest to this; there are 2 million black American communicants in the Roman Catholic Church.[4] However, roughly 80 percent of black Christians call one of the seven black denominations home. And so a solid portrait of the religious life of black Christians is captured through attention to the African Methodist Episcopal Church; the African Methodist Episcopal Zion Church; the Christian Methodist Episcopal Church; the National Baptist Convention, U.S.A., Inc.; the National

Baptist Convention of America; the Progressive National Baptist Convention; and the Church of God in Christ.

Black Christians represent a full range of socioeconomic groups. In recent years more young people (18-35 years of age) have renewed their relationship with the major denominations, although the percentage of women has remained disproportionately high. The largest denominations all report that women make up 60-70 percent of the total membership. These churches also report that the vast majority of their local congregations, as of the early twentieth century, were located in urban areas. While it is difficult at best to calculate the income of individual church members, recent estimates noted that the median income for urban churches in the early 1980s ranged from $15,000 per year to $25,000.[5]

Some 25 million black Christians across the nation engage in worship each week for the same reasons. And they would agree, for the most part, that what happens Sunday, during service, influences their activities during the week and informs their outlook on socioeconomic, cultural, and political realities. That is to say, worship and the beliefs that inform it are more than the passive expression of faith. To the contrary, they constitute a major impetus for praxis extending beyond church walls. Although worship grounded in theological assumptions has not always borne sociopolitical fruit, at its best the Black Church has been concerned with both the mystery of Christ and with the worldly struggle for freedom and equality. As historian Gayraud Wilmore puts it,

> Black religion has always concerned itself with the fascination of an incorrigibly religious people with the mystery of God, but it has been equally concerned with the yearning of a despised and subjugated people for freedom—freedom from the religious, economic, social, and political domination that whites have exercised over blacks since the beginning of the African slave trade. It is this radical thrust of blacks for human liberation expressed in theological terms and *religious institutions* that is the defining characteristic of black Christianity and black religion in the United States (emphasis added).[6]

Much of what has transpired in this country with respect to civil rights and social betterment has been envisioned and orchestrated by lay Christians and their pastors. According to a recent study conducted by sociologist Andrew Billingsley, most churches maintain some type of outreach emphasis addressing the pressing needs of their particular communities.

The number of outreach programs sponsored was proportionate to the size (and one can assume resource base) of the congregation: the larger the church the more outreach programs sponsored.[7] Whether individual members would label themselves activists or not is difficult to say, but what is more certain is the manner in which black churches for a good portion of their history have engaged the pressing issues of the day, often in cooperation with one another and secular agencies such as the National Association for the Advancement of Colored People (NAACP) and governmental agencies.

From the debate over slavery to the civil rights movement, black churches and their ministers have shaped the way political figures and the public view race relations. This commitment to the welfare of humanity is premised on an embrace of the social gospel—the impact of Christian principles on daily life. The basic premise of the Black Church suggests service to God and to the human community through attention to the liberating affects of the gospel message. That is to say, black churches are marked by a tentative positioning between two worlds, giving attention to both—the secular and the sacred. They have provided a full range of services from salvation to social services. These churches have developed, in large part, as a response to discrimination that affected both worship and work. Yet black Christianity as expressed through black churches is in no sense limited to political and social activities. These churches recognize a divine motivation for their activities in that the word of God requires spiritual and material freedom. Put another way, humans were created by God for freedom, as subjects not objects. In this sense it might be wise to frame an investigation of black Christianity as expressed by black churches in terms of confrontation between secular demands and sacred promises—expressed in the language of the holy.

Charles Long, a historian of religions who has done ground-breaking work on the nature of religion and religious meaning in the Americas, offers a useful definition of religion in his book *Significations*: "Religion will mean orientation—orientation in the ultimate sense, that is, how one comes to terms with the ultimate significance of one's place in the world. . . . The religion of any people is more than a structure of thought; it is experience, expression, motivations, intentions, behavior, styles, and rhythms."[8] Drawing from Long, religion among black Christians houses a quest for meaning, an effort to makes sense of human interactions in light of the divine and through this process to achieve some form of liberation. As Long writes: "The situation of the cultures of black peoples in the United States afforded a religious experience of radical otherness, a resourceful and critical moment that allowed these communities to undertake radical internal criticisms of themselves, their situation, and the situation of the majority culture."[9] Christianity within black American communities provides orientation and direction for life within a world that often appears absurd because of its racism. From this religion blacks have gained a sense of self-worth and connection to God that counter attempts to define them as inferior because of skin color.

Black religion, in the form of Christianity, entails an approach to living in the world haunted by a divine imperative, an effort to make sense of certain experiences in light of sacred promises. This commitment echoed throughout the history, doctrine, worship, and outreach of black churches marks the essential elements of black Christianity in the past and the contemporary period. Although black churches have at times faltered with respect to this mission, they are concerned with the full range of human needs—spiritual renewal and the demands for a comfortable life. At times this has entailed an embrace of social rules and regulations; in other cases Christianity within black American communities has entailed a bold rejection of social rules and regulations. This process of biblically based protest begins with the secret gatherings of enslaved Africans called hush-arbor meetings or the invisible institution and continues today in the form of established churches found in cities throughout the United States. This is a complex and multi-layered history, bits and pieces of which have been captured in many volumes housed on library shelves across the country. But how might a snapshot of this Black Church look, particularly when it is primarily concerned with capturing the essence and activism of the Black Church over the past few decades? The purpose of this book is to provide such a snap shot. In this sense it is an introduction to black Christianity through attention to the history of its thought, practices, and activism.

This volume is divided into two sections, the first section (chapters 1-3) describes themes in the history of the Black Church as well as major beliefs and the forms of worship that define the Black Church Tradition. It is important to present this information because it provides the historical, theological, and ritual context for the praxis discussed in the second section of the book.[10] And, if praxis in fact entails the joining of reflection and action, this first section seeks to provide some sense of the Black Church's reflection (theological and historical sensibilities as well as ritual) while the second addresses the Black Church's actions (and points of inactivity). It is only in this way, by attention to both its reflection and its activism, that one gains a sense of the Black Church's praxis. Within the section on activism, chapter 4 covers issues related to economics, such as poverty and environmental racism. The next chapter covers the Black Church and its response to health issues and sexuality.

Perhaps the most pressing internal dilemma facing the Black Church across denominational lines has been, and continues to be, the full inclusion of black women and what this means with respect to doctrine and ministry in the broadest sense of the word. Women represent the majority of Black Church membership, yet this is not reflected in the positions of authority held by women. This dilemma is discussed in chapter 6. The final chapter provides a brief comment on two related concerns within Black Church circles. They are the growth in black "megachurches" and the use of new technologies. In highlighting this phenomenon, this chapter outlines the impact of recent technological advances on church ministry (and audience) as well as perceptions of the Black Church's continuing presence in black communities: What does it mean to do ministry with a twelve-thousand-member congregation? What does it mean to conduct outreach with a congregation that is heavily based on TV viewership and Internet information? What is the relationship between the Church's prior commitment to a social gospel and the "gospel of prosperity" espoused by many megachurches?

Following the discussion of megachurches and technology, the volume concludes with a chronology and list of resources for further study. In addition to highlighting some sources used in completing this volume, the list is intended to be "reader friendly" by supplying a full range of annotated materials for review—videos and websites, as well as books and journals.

My depiction of the Black Church highlights the important and creative tension between "spiritual" and "mundane" concerns to which churches respond and by which churches are shaped. In short, the assumptions that guide this project are very much in line with the questions and concerns that guide liberation theology, my area of academic specialization: spiritual renewal, social justice, and liberation as the fundamental business of religious organizations. Scholarly texts; case studies (by the author and others); the Internet, popular press, and church documents are all used to provide a complex portrait of churches as they are viewed externally and as they are viewed by committed church members. In constructing this text, an effort has been made to include comments from church leaders and laity in order to provide an "insider" perspective and additional texture to the project. Addressed to students with little to no knowledge of the subject as well as general readers, I hope that this book will foster a deeper understanding of one of the more powerful and influential structures of black religious experience—the Black Church.

PART I

HISTORICAL AND THEOLOGICAL BACKGROUND

Dexter Ave. Baptist Church
Montgomery, Alabama
(This was Martin Luther King Jr.'s church
during the Montgomery bus boycott.)

Themes in Black Church History, 1864 to 1970

The history of the Black Church is complex and multilayered, and develops in response to a blending of sociopolitical, economic, cultural, and religious factors that are intensified by the fight over the fate of the union. From the perspective of black Christians from Methodist and Baptist churches, the Civil War and Reconstruction were signs of God's displeasure with the system of slavery as well as God's call for the evangelizing of the elusive South. Missionary work was difficult because of limited access to transportation and harassment from those who did not want southern society changed by northern sensibilities. Former slave owners, and many white Northerners who moved to the South, were determined to maintain the codes and social relationships in place before the invasion of the North. This meant missionaries who "traveled much beyond the security of Federal soldiers almost anywhere in the South . . . exposed themselves to danger."[1] As missionary Hiram Revels remarks, physical harm remained a possibility even after the war: "It is an undisguised fact that no man can safely go beyond the lines of the Freedmen's Bureau, without endangering his life."[2] Even when missionaries did not encounter open hostility, it was not uncommon for them to lack resources necessary for their fledgling churches to have a house of worship. In these cases preaching the gospel had to be combined with a business sense and construction skills. In other cases appropriate space was available but it was necessary to secure it through creative means. For instance, with limited success some black missionaries argued that Confederate whites had surrendered their rights to church buildings by abandoning them during the war. And it was only right that these churches be used by freed blacks because they had been built by and often used exclusively by blacks.[3]

Despite the difficulties, growth occurred. Increase in membership, however, was usually hard fought in that much of this period (the Civil War and Reconstruction) was marked by feuds between blacks of different denominations over potential members. For example, it was not uncommon for Baptist ministers to lampoon the rigidity of ritual and education preoccupation for ministry espoused by Daniel Payne of the AME Church. And in turn, Methodists would often make light of the lack of formal organization and "style" found in Baptist churches. Methodists tried to differentiate themselves by pointing to the orderly style of worship in their churches, while Baptists were charged with being far too energetic in worship. In addition, Methodist evangelists often accused Baptists of being uneducated and socially unrefined. Ministers in black churches, regardless of denomination, typically represented the "elite" of black society, with greater economic and social clout than others. But this was not always the result of formal education or status due to bloodlines in the "correct" family. Both Methodist and Baptist churches contained a good number of ministers who had been slaves or were born to enslaved parents. Hence, the success of these ministers was more likely tied to preaching ability and strong connections to black communities.

Regardless of this fighting between denominations, the recently freed sought out opportunity to join these churches because they were symbols of black independence. Blacks saw membership in these churches as an opportunity to express their new citizenship as well as a venue by which to give more visible expression to their deeply seated religious convictions. Black Methodist and Baptist churches also provided opportunity to exercise leadership skills that had been circumscribed by the slave system.

The Church and Its Relationship to Africa

Growth in numbers, resources, and institutional infrastructure allowed the Black Church to extend its gaze beyond the United States. The Church was not content to only preach the gospel on familiar soil, recognizing that Africa must be redeemed. According to most black Christians this meant the spreading of the Christian faith to the continent of Africa in keeping with God's will. Using funds raised largely by black women, churches began sending missionaries to Africa in the early 1800s. For example, in 1820, Daniel Coker of the AME Church became the first black Methodist missionary to Africa when he left Baltimore for Liberia, West Africa. One year later Lott Carey joined Coker in Liberia, thereby becoming the first black Baptist missionary to Africa.[4] Missionaries had a difficult time adjusting to the difference in climate, culture, and social relationships that marked Africa. Illness and dwindling resources often resulted in missionaries returning to America having accomplished less than they had hoped. In other cases the inability to speak the native languages hindered missions. As AME minister Levi Coppin notes, "Those missionaries who have studied the native tongues—of which there are many—and translated the Bible in the vernacular of various tribes, have done a work that is of inestimable value. The difficulty of language is, after all, the greatest hardship in evangelistic work in Africa."[5] When missionaries learned the necessary languages and translated Bibles and other materials into those languages, they made some progress toward spreading the gospel. Most did so through church services and the development of schools that provided basic reading and writing as well as indoctrination into the Christian faith. By the 1960s black Methodist denominations and Baptist conventions claimed more than 2 million members in Africa. Black Pentecostals as represented by the Church of God in Christ (COGIC), because they developed during the early twentieth century, would not enter foreign missions until the mid-twentieth century. Accurate information on the size of African membership for COGIC is unavailable, although most scholars acknowledge that it is "well represented overseas, particularly in Africa and the Caribbean."[6]

Black Christians in large numbers believed that God set them aside and prepared them to bring the gospel to Africans. But some went further with this reasoning and argued that this must include more than spotty missionary work. It must entail a form of black nationalism that generated the development of a new country populated by Africans and black Americans who emigrated back to Africa. Only in Africa would blacks gain their self-esteem and fulfill their socioeconomic and religious potential given them by God. For advocates of this position the United States was meant by God to be only a training ground, not a permanent home. This perspective was commonly justified theologically by arguing that God had allowed the enslavement of Africans in order to fit them with the Christian faith and an understanding of democratic government. Once this information was secured, they were to take it back to Africa. They saw this as the fulfillment of scripture—"and Ethiopia shall stretch forth her hands unto God" (Ps 68:31)—that spoke to Africa regaining God's favor and thereby its former glory. Ministers and laity who believed this often took their cue from Episcopal priest and early advocate of emigration (the Back-to-Africa movement) Alexander Crummell. Regarding the need for permanent relocation Crummell says in 1865:

> If you send a missionary to Africa, you send, indeed, a good, holy, faithful minister; but he is but an individual; he may, or he may not, plant Christianity in the field. The probability is that he will not; for the greatest of saints can only represent a partial Christianity. Hence the likelihood, the almost certainty is, that his work will have to be followed up by others. When, therefore, you send a single individual, as a missionary, you do not necessarily send Christianity to Africa; albeit you send a devoted Christian. On the other hand, when you send out a company of Christian emigrants, you send a church.[7]

The appeal of this emigrationist agenda as set by Crummell, AME bishop Henry McNeal Turner, and numerous others was limited primarily to a small group dominated by southern blacks whose life in rural areas suggested no escape from poverty and racism except by emigration. However, talk of unmatched economic opportunity in Africa did not translate into actual gain but did allow for the expansion of black churches. An example of this is the Liberian Exodus Joint Stock Steamship Company developed in 1877. According to historian Lawrence Little:

> stockholders raised enough to buy a ship, the Azor, characterized by [Martin] Delany as the "African Mayflower." In 1878, several families and individuals including AME missionary Simon F. Flegler emigrated to West Africa. Although lack of money and preparedness doomed the colonizers and forced investors to sell the ship, the venture provided missionaries the opportunity to establish the church in West Africa. . . . The enterprise, however, revealed the hardships involved in trying to establish African emigration as a viable solution to the social, political, and economic problems of African Americans.[8]

The Back-to-Africa agenda would lose its appeal during the early twentieth century because of such hardships, lack of finances, and the death in 1915 of its major spokesperson, Henry McNeal Turner. It would surface again, with no greater success, through Marcus Garvey and his Universal Negro Improvement Association, brought to the United States in 1916. Garvey's work represented the largest mass movement of black Americans in the history of the United States, but it lacked the formal links to the Black Church represented by the earlier Back-to-Africa movement.

Those not interested in the Back-to-Africa movement saw the Civil War and Reconstruction as a real push on the part of the United States to move beyond racism and provide full citizenship to blacks. But blacks would have to prove themselves worthy. Often torn between W. E. B. Du Bois's demand for participation in U.S. life on all levels—political, cultural, social, and economic—and Booker T. Washington's emphasis on economic inclusion through self-help, the Black Church pushed blacks to apply the morals and ethics found in scripture to every aspect of life. They saw the Church as the best hope for blacks in that it provided a "safe" space in which to discuss and work on both their spiritual and material standing.

The Great Migration and Religious Diversification

In addition to the planting of new churches, this dual purpose—spiritual and material development—often spurred the development of kindergartens, libraries, savings banks, schools, and other resources that allowed the recently freed blacks to enter American society as informed and useful citizens. While always important, these programs and institutions gained greater importance with the quick urbanization of black Americans at the turn of the century. Black denominations in existence near the close of the nineteenth century were forever changed by what is commonly called the Great Migration, beginning during the late years of the nineteenth century and continuing through the first three decades of the twentieth century. To give some sense of the numbers involved, by 1920 roughly 500,000 black Americans moved to the North, and by 1930 more than 1.5 million had moved out of the South.[9] Whites, afraid of the potential economic and social ramifications of this mass movement, attempted to coerce black Americans into remaining in the South. Yet, in spite of the often hostile—legal and extralegal—white resistance and some reluctance on the part of black leaders such as Frederick Douglass and numerous black church leaders, the motivation for moving was far too great.

Black Americans had limited economic opportunities; they were usually restricted to tenant and sharecropping farm positions, in which they increased their debt to white landowners while accruing minimal profits at best. According to noted historian John Hope Franklin, black farm workers in South Carolina, for example, made only $10.79 in pay each month compared to the $26.13 a month earned by workers in New

York. Furthermore, in terms of land ownership, at the turn of the century black Americans possessed fewer than 159,000 farms throughout the South, while white farmers owned more than 1,078,600.[10] Those who gained a measure of success faced the hostility of white mobs—including the destruction of businesses and/or lynching—angered by economic achievement of an "inferior" group. This hostility was usually justified by tradition as well as a series of "Jim Crow" regulations making equality not only socially unacceptable but also unlawful.

Black Americans made their way to northern cities where, by the early twentieth century, job opportunities were promised due to the war effort (World War I). However, upon reaching cities such as Chicago, migrants found themselves relegated to inner-city slums, paying higher rents than the available non-labor union jobs afforded. Racial bias prevented them from achieving the economic success they believed would be available in the "promised land," and close confinement in ghettos resulted in health problems. What is more, few recreational opportunities and limited access to green spaces often meant increased juvenile delinquency. In short, black Americans faced social, political, and economic hardship based on a continuing legacy of discrimination.

This mass movement was a mixed blessing for black denominations. Whereas many denominations, as of Reconstruction, held most of their membership in the South, the migration meant the growth of church memberships in the North. But this growth came at the expense of their southern conferences and state conventions, which experienced a decline in membership as black Methodists and Baptists made their way north in search of better jobs. This was particularly hard on rural churches that were typically small even prior to the Great Migration. As the *Southern Standard* remarked in 1916, "Many of the churches cannot have meetings where there have been the largest attendance, and some of the preachers say that they cannot get congregations enough to have service, for the reason that those who have not left are saving up money to go with."[11] Some ministers tried to dissuade blacks from moving, but such arguments were of little success in the face of mounting economic hardship and social disenfranchisement. Other ministers, like R. H. Harmon of Mississippi, moved North themselves, taking with them as many church members as possible. In reflecting on his move to Chicago, Harmon said: "I am working at my trade. I have saved enough to bring my wife and four children and some of my congregation. We are here for keeps."[12]

Migrants who did not travel with an intact congregation maintained membership in churches in the South and tried as best they could to continue their financial support of church work "back home." Others sought out new churches, assuming that the North had to contain black

Christians of similar religious orientation and perspective on life in the United States. The transition, however, was hardly smooth. Established churches had internal issues that took up a great deal of time and attention. The continuing threat of schisms within Baptist conventions resulting from issues of autonomy and collaboration with white Baptist organizations, for example, stymied an embrace of emigrants. Methodist denominations considered uniting in order to better serve existing religious and social needs, but disagreement on how to arrange bishops and departments prevented any type of merger from actually occurring. In addition, both Baptist and Methodist churches concerned themselves with the trappings of middle-class status and a conservative gospel of personal purification from sin. For many of these denominations, emigrants brought to the more sophisticated North unrefined and emotional styles of religious worship and sensibilities reeking from the residue of slave culture. Those in the North prior to this Great Migration had made necessary adjustments and had embraced socially acceptable (read: assimilationist) religious formats in keeping with the sensibilities and aspirations of a growing black bourgeoisie—those in the black community whose jobs as skilled laborers, teachers, governmental employees, and artisans gave them a measure of economic stability and comfort. Having gained some measure of acceptance and success, black churches and their leaders by and large did not want their progress hampered by a new membership that reminded them and the larger white society of blacks during slavery, who were stereotyped as ignorant, backward, and culturally insignificant.

Even when established churches embraced emigrants, there were conditions attached. Most notably, longstanding members of these black churches assumed that they would continue to play the lead in black social and religious life. This North *vs.* South control of denominations did not begin with the migration, but it did amplify the friction between the two camps. The AME Church expressed this growing concern with respect to the migration's impact on church hierarchy. According to historian Milton Sernett:

> Since the Civil War, southern black Methodists had increased their numbers disproportionately to northern constituents in the national bodies. Yet they lacked parity in the inner circles of power. Intersectional struggles resulted. The election and addition of bishops to episcopal councils frequently became battles over regional influence. Southerners wanted a greater voice in church affairs, which had been dominated by northern-based bishops whose influence derived from pre-Civil War ecclesiastical arrangements.[13]

As the number of Southerners in the churches increased, leaders had to give more attention to their demands for full participation in the workings of the churches. Prior to the migration, the center of membership for black denominations was in the South. The migration shifted this to the North and thereby had strong ramifications for the way geographic considerations affected the election of Methodist church leaders. In addition, mass movement of blacks meant a rethinking of where church resources should go, where new churches should be built, where ministers should serve, and how conferences and associations should be developed on the regional level. Baptists also felt the strain. They had historically concentrated their mission efforts in the South, but the migration required a rethinking of this focus. Southern churches were decreasing in size and financial resources, and migrant Baptists in the North were struggling to establish themselves. Schisms during this period and continuing friction weakened Baptist institutional structures and hampered efforts to raise funds for northern missions. Under these conditions, even ministers and churches anxious to help emigrants found it difficult to do so.

Newly arrived blacks found their way into established Methodist and Baptist churches. Others sought fellowship within Episcopal, Congregational, Presbyterian, and Roman Catholic churches. And still others developed their own religious organizations or entered more marginal religious communities in which their religious and cultural sensibilities were welcomed and nurtured. Within this landscape of religious bodies, the most notable development might be Pentecostalism, a religious movement started during the nineteenth century as the United States attempted to recover from the Civil War and its socioeconomic, political, and cultural ramifications (for example, intensified racial conflict and violence). Pentecostalism, as exemplified in black denominations such as the Church of God in Christ, has its roots in an earlier holiness movement defined by emotional worship, a literal interpretation of scripture, belief in healing, and a doctrine of salvation as available to all.

The Black Church's Social Gospel: Jesus and Jobs

The Great Migration during which the Church of God in Christ developed has already been mentioned, but waves of movement continued through the 1960s for similar reasons. Estimates run as high as 4 million black Americans moving to western and northern cities over the three decades from 1940 to 1970, resulting in more than half of the total black population living in urban areas.[14] The geographic rearrangement of the black population meant a radical shift from agricultural occupations to blue-collar industrial jobs and service-related work. But by 1954 this shift had proven of little economic benefit. For example, the unemployment ratio between blacks and whites was 2 to 1. And the average income for a black American male was roughly 70 percent that of a white male. And for black women and white women it was even less, with black women being the poorest paid of the four groups. Whites in large numbers moved to the suburbs, while immigrants and blacks forged an existence out of the decaying structures, limited resources, and substandard jobs available to inner-city dwellers. There was a growing and seemingly permanent under-class and black Americans were a part of it. In the words of political scientist Manning Marable, the flip side of America's development was the intentional "underdevelopment of black America," nurtured by mutating frameworks that served to exclude most from the avenues of success, leaving in their wake frustration, hopelessness, and nihilism.[15] Black churches were growing in status in some circles based on middle-class membership as well as the more general stability that comes with age. Yet most blacks remained economically strapped and without necessary political clout to improve this situation significantly. Did the decline in the number of ministers within the black community during this period signal an overall drop in the Church's status that marred its ability to influence the national agenda? Were the Church's critics correct in arguing that clergy and the churches they represented were self-serving peddlers of "feel good-isms" that served only to maintain the status quo?

Whereas many local churches chose a conservative path of limited resistance to social arrangements, others turned activist and participated in a struggle for equality that changed American society. Even before the beginning of the formal civil rights movement, ministers like Reverdy C. Ransom (AME), Walter Hood (AMEZ), and L. K. Williams (Baptist) worked to keep their churches active in the overall development of black communities during the Great Migration. Placing their ministries within the framework of the social gospel, they argued that Christianity had social implications that required Christians to work toward the ending of poverty and racial discrimination. Ransom's response to critiques of his Institutional AME Church contains the sense of mission and purpose common to all black social gospellers of the period:

> The Institutional AME Church of Chicago was not born before its time. It comes to meet and serve the social conditions and industrial needs of the people, and to give answers and solutions to the many grave problems which confront our Christianity in the great

centers of population of our people. It is not a dream spun out of the gossamer web of fancy; it is not an evasion, an abridgment, or a short-cut method for the realization of Christ and the Christ life in the life of the people. It is a teaching, ministering nursing-mother, and seeks through its activities and ministrations to level the inequalities and bridge the chasms between rich and poor, the educated and the ignorant, the virtuous and the vicious, the indolent and the thrifty, the vulgar and the refined, and to bring all ages and classes of the community to contribute to the common good.[16]

Ransom urged the Black Church to live out the social ramifications of the gospel of Christ, in keeping with its own rhetoric. Reflecting on this within the context of the AME Church, he says:

At every level of the Connection and in every local church, the African Methodist Episcopal Church shall engage in carrying out the spirit of the original Free African Society, out of which the A.M.E. Church evolved: that is, to seek out and save the lost, and serve the needy through a continuing program of (1) preaching the gospel, (2) feeding the hungry, (3) clothing the naked, (4) housing the homeless, (5) cheering the fallen, (6) providing jobs for the jobless, (7) administering to the needs of those in prisons, hospitals, nursing homes, asylums and mental institutions, senior citizens' homes; caring for the sick, the shut-in, the mentally and socially disturbed, and (8) encouraging thrift and economic advancement.[17]

To accomplish this, many black churches developed a variety of social services including libraries, job training, basic education programs, and health-care programs. And these activities on the part of black churches speak to an appreciation for a social form of Christianity that is sensitive to the changing cultural and social realities encountered by black Americans and is willing to break the boundaries of "tradition" in order to accomplish this larger objective. One of the best mid-twentieth century examples of this attitude is Adam Clayton Powell, Jr., of Abyssinian Baptist Church in New York City. As a high-profile minister and Harlem's first black congressman (1944-69), Powell fought for black Americans and pointed to a form of social gospel that blended the best of the Christian tradition with the wisdom of the streets. This combination is evident in his often quoted line, "Keep the faith, baby."[18] Using strategies of public protest that became the hallmark of the civil rights movement, Powell secured jobs in white-owned Harlem stores, worked for better health care, and brought some order to a tense and potentially explosive section of New York. Powell's legacy, however, was not simply based on jobs secured, public spaces desegregated, and social tensions addressed during the 1930s and early 1940s. As a politician first in the city council and then in Congress (1944), he became chair of the influential House Committee on Education and Labor in 1961. And from this position he worked on legislation meant to improve the life chances of forgotten Americans through educational and economic reform.

The Church and the Civil Rights Movement

Social gospel inspired ministers, such as Ransom and Powell, represented rather isolated protest as opposed to large scale and more denominationally focused programs. Most churches in black denominations lacked the leadership, vision, and resources necessary for such multi-leveled ministries. It was not until the civil rights movement that there developed a persistent and collective cooperation on national issues of injustice and discrimination. Through participation in this push for social transformation and political change, black churches and their leaders came full circle. And, in addition to providing bodies willing to participate in direct action, disseminate information, and finance protest activities, the Black Church also provided the ideological and theological underpinning for the movement.

By all accounts, the civil rights movement begins with the Montgomery (Alabama) Bus Boycott of 1955-56. This, of course, was not the first attempt at nonviolent direct action for promoting social change. The work of Powell as well as students who, during the 1940s, staged various sit-ins predates the Montgomery action. Nonetheless, the consequences of the bus boycott were far-reaching. With Rosa Parks's arrest for not surrendering her seat on a public bus, a boycott was called for and the Baptist Ministerial Alliance in Montgomery responded by becoming part of the leadership base referred to as the Montgomery Improvement Association (MIA). From the work of this organization and its member churches, the struggle for equal access to public transportation grew into a movement for civil rights across the United States.

Under the leadership of Martin L. King, Jr., the civil rights movement drew on the "truth-force" philosophy of Indian leader Gandhi and the social gospel to move away from the Church's complacency of the early twentieth century and to reconnect with the social agenda that framed the work of the first generation of independent black churches. This shift in the Church's priorities was modeled by ministers and, although many church leaders refused to participate, according to civil rights activist Jo

Ann Robinson, "the ministers gave themselves, their time . . . and their leadership . . . which set examples for the laymen to follow. They gave us confidence, faith in ourselves, faith in them and their leadership, that helped the congregations to support the movement every foot of the way."[19] There is no doubt that these ministers played a vital role. But Robinson's comment also suggests that the mission established by King and other prominent figures in the civil rights movement required the active participation of congregations. Members of churches created and distributed information, raised money, spread word of meetings, boycotted businesses, and marched in accordance with the vision of freedom presented by the movement's leadership.

Mass meetings and Sunday services played a major role in securing the participation of black Christians. For instance, King speaks to the importance of church members in the work of the Montgomery bus boycott: "A mass meeting was being held that night. There I asked all those who were willing to offer their cars to give us their names, addresses, telephone numbers, and the hours that they could drive, before leaving the meeting. The response was tremendous. . . . The ministers agreed to go to their pulpits the following day and seek additional recruits. Again the response was tremendous. With the new additions, the number of cars swelled to about three hundred."[20] Even when pulpits were not used to secure volunteers, black churches provided information that shaped the political actions of congregants. As Mary Fair Burks, a member of the Baptist church and founder of the Women's Political Council active during the Montgomery Bus Boycott, remarks: "As chairman of the Political Action Committee of the Dexter Avenue Baptist church—a committee formed by Dr. King—following church services I would read the names of the candidates whom we had decided were the least objectionable, considering the fact that we would be voting under the slogan 'White Supremacy.' Other churches initiated similar practices."[21] Through this process black churches sought to create voting blocs that reinforced the direct action activities of the movement. Through participation in this boycott and other protest campaigns, black Christians practiced their noncompliance with oppressive social customs and racist laws, and secured the role of the Black Church in the movement.

The Black Church on Black Power

The Black Church faced a major challenge to its faith-based activism when members of the Student Nonviolent Coordinating Committee (SNCC) became disillusioned with nonviolent direct action strategy. This shift in ideology was captured in the phrase *Black Power*, which spoke to a growing black consciousness embracing new and more radical approaches to social transformation. Black Power meant a turn from illusionary cooperation with whites, whose liberalism could only promote limited systemic change. From the first conference held in 1967, Black Power involved an embrace of self-determination, a critical read of history, and a new vision of economic and political power. In short, it was white power confronted by a determined force. White liberals and the media were shocked by their exclusion, but Black Power advocates were sending a clear message: this struggle is not about you—whites—it's about the welfare of black people, and only black people can set the agenda! The civil rights movement, Black Power advocates argued, had come to an end, leaving behind much unfinished business.

Some within church circles denounced the Black Power movement as being grounded in dangerous ideology and inflammatory rhetoric that ran contrary to more popular calls for tolerance and brotherhood. Others were unwilling to be so dismissive and instead attempted to reconcile the Christian principles of the civil rights movement with the Malcolm X–inspired demands for Black Power. A major outgrowth of this perspective was the 1966 ad hoc committee formed by the National Council of Churches' Benjamin Payton and a host of ministers representing various denominations. This group was called the National Committee of Negro Churchmen (NCNC). In its early published platform the organization attempted to interpret Black Power in light of the Christian gospel and in this way harness the energy and anger of young people throughout the country.[22] The organization depicted the riots and other 1960s events as a minor threat to national security, the major threat being a failure of the nation to live in accordance with God's demand for justice and righteousness. This was the first statement on Black Power issued by members of the Black Church, and its impact was far-reaching in that it did more than just provide a theological justification for Black Power. It was an assertion of the Black Church's relevance in the struggle for a liberated existence.

As the 1960s came to an end, however, the vast majority of the nation's black churches lost their commitment to social activism. This retreat from progressive politics was amplified by the murder of Martin L. King, Jr., in 1968. In the words of James Cone, one of the early figures in the development of black theology: "The lack of vision in the churches is mirrored in the civil rights movement because the two have been and are closely related. . . . With many persons wanting to be leaders and few wanting to follow, and with many leaders more concerned about their media image than about creating the structures for the liberation of the poor, it becomes clear why there have been no new visions."[23] This redirecting of the Church's focus and the appeal to the individualism that marked the theology of many ministers resulted in a public relations nightmare for the Church. As the 1970s got under way, the Black Church began to feel the consequences of its turn toward political and social conservatism as black Americans looked to other organizations for guidance and support.

Butler Chapel
AME Zion Church
Tuskegee, Alabama

2

Themes in Black Church History, 1970 to the Present

Although the Black Church had faltered on its promise to address the needs of black Americans during much of the early twentieth century, it had during the civil rights movement emerged as a vital factor in the sociopolitical and economic life of the United States. Church leaders argued during the turbulent years between 1955 and 1968 that the Christian faith, if applied to social ills, could transform the nation. Baptist minister and intellectual Benjamin E. Mays points to this hope when saying that "the battle will not be easy but those who believe in Jesus, in God, in justice, and in equality cannot and will not retreat. Upon complete victory in this area, hangs the welfare of all mankind."[1] Black Christians from a variety of denominations and conventions took seriously this call to battle against discrimination based upon a vision of human equality. Church leaders often received the media attention, but the sit-ins, boycotts, marches, and meetings were made possible in large part by the sacrifices and energies of church laity.

Black churches provided the "foot soldiers" for this battle and in this way made a claim for being a "place of power both within the black community and as the black community's representative in the white society."[2] Once again, the Black Church presented itself as the strongest institution for social reform within black communities, and church members used the history and insights of this institution to act in the world. Civil rights activist Ella Baker speaks to this Church-based activism. In reflecting on her motivation for activism, she said: "My grandfather had gone into the Baptist ministry, and that was part of the quote, unquote,

Christian concept of sharing with others. I went to a school that went in for Christian training. Then, there were people who 'stood for something,' as I call it. Your relationship to human beings was more important than your relationship to the amount of money that you made."[3] Others like Baker served on the front lines of the civil rights struggle as well as serving in other capacities.

This blending of social protest and Christian faith resulted in many scholars, preachers, and laypeople thinking of the Black Church and black communities as intimately connected. This points to an important and historical intertwining of the Black Church's development and the needs of black Americans, which probably hit its twentieth-century high point with the civil rights movement. The next two decades, the 1970s and 1980s, however, call into question this assumed overlapping of identities. As Baptist minister Dennis W. Wiley notes: "Quiet as it is kept, this identity between the Black Church and the African-American community is now probably more myth than reality. The Black Church and the African community are not identical, and the gap between them is growing wider every day."[4] Mindful of this and what it could mean in terms of the survival of local congregations as well as the threat it poses to the Black Church Tradition as a whole, black churches spent much of the past three decades rethinking membership and mission in light of late-twentieth-century socioeconomic and political realities faced by black Americans.

The Black Church in Decline, 1970s–1980s

Political Passivity and Secularization

The 1970s marked a general decline in the reputation of black churches because the end of the civil rights movement and the rise of more radical and nationalistic orientations brought into question the merit of church involvement. Many churches fueled this questioning through a declining interest in areas of civil leadership once embraced.[5] The Black Church had gone through a similar period of "otherworldliness" during the Great Migration, when it surrendered much of its social activism to organizations such as the National Association for the Advancement of Colored People. However, in the civil rights movement black denominations seemed to regain their progressive politics and activism only to lose this thrust at the end of the 1960s.

An earlier concern for social justice seemed lost to a new sense of individual pietism that promised heaven but did little to change the existential situation of black Americans. The Church's 300-year-long struggle with oppression in this country seemed futile for many who saw no real progress made, while the Black Church became richer and its ministers more comfortable with middle-class status. According to one Baptist minister, "Instead of cursing the white man, [blacks] shout at the Lord. Instead of kicking whitey, [blacks] kick over the pew."[6] One of the more controversial critics, political scientist Adolph Reed, links the hyper-spirituality lamented by the above minister to the sociopolitical complacency of black Americans who are under the influence of black churches. Expressing the frustration of many, he says that "the domain of the black church has been the spiritual and institutional adaptation of Afro-Americans to an apparently inexorable context of subordination and dispossession."[7]

With regard to the public struggle for equality, the Church had little to say. In other words, as Beverly Hall Lawrence observes:

> On college campuses, middle-class blacks were embracing a kind of intellectual and cultural attitude called black nationalism. At the same time, in urban centers, the black consciousness movement with its slogans . . . was attracting followers with the same spirit of nationalism. Black Americans' cultural soul was on fire as well, and all our symbols were being questioned—including the white Jesus that we had bowed before during our childhood. My generation was one that fled churches filled with those who appeared to us to be helpless.[8]

This disregard for the Church continued and seems akin to a general U.S. trend toward secularization. Concerning this, the middle class affirmed in practice what law professor Stephen L. Carter recently labeled an attempt to push religious belief to the fringes of public exchanges. Concisely put, public discourse on issues of "secular" concern attempted to treat

> religious beliefs as arbitrary and unimportant, a trend supported by a rhetoric that implied that there is something wrong with religious devotion. More and more, our culture seems to take the position that believing deeply in the tenets of one's faith represents a kind of mystical irrationality, something that thoughtful, public-spirited American citizens would do better to avoid. If you must worship your God, the lesson runs, at least have the courtesy to disbelieve in the power of prayer; if you must observe your sabbath, have the

good sense to understand that it is just like any other day off from work.[9]

According to Carter, much energy has been given to downplaying the practice of religious faith for fear such practice might interfere with the workings of society and, even worse, compromise our democratic vision. Such a claim, when embraced by black Americans, had to affect the Church and deflate its membership.

Theories of Black Church decline in reputation and in some cases membership during the past several decades are not limited to talk of disgruntled baby boomers, who are disillusioned with the demise of the civil rights movement. In fact, there is a large segment of the black community too young to have memories of the civil rights movement, but who were born during the disillusionment of the 1980s. Almost 53 percent of all black Americans in 1998 were under 30, with nearly 40 percent under 20.[10] According to Robert Franklin, former professor at Emory University and current president of the Interdenominational Theological Center: "Barely three decades after the movement began, the black church is in decline. . . . A generation ago, four out of every five inner city black men had some contact with church or Sunday school. Today [1995], studies show three out of five have no church contact whatsoever."[11] These children were born during a period when the Black Church was held suspect and their attitude often reflects this perspective. As Rev. Jamal Harrison Bryant, who was appointed youth director for the NAACP in 1997, argues: "A lot of them don't have an idea of how they can be socially active in the 1990s. [They see] the civil rights movement as, 'Oh, that's what happened in Selma, Montgomery, Jackson and the March on Washington.' They don't understand that civil rights is yet a struggle even today."[12] And, furthermore, they have little reason to believe the Black Church is active in contemporary struggles. Even when churches tried to address young people through full-time youth pastors or youth ministers, their function tended to revolve around the creation of recreational opportunities rather than pressing late-twentieth-century problems such as gang activity.[13]

This perspective has been forcefully presented in popular culture in the form of hip hop. Examples abound, but one of the more telling, from my perspective, is the song "Fishin' 4 Religion" recorded by the early 1990s' sensation Arrested Development. In this song the group critiques the lack of sociopolitical vision found in black churches, arguing that ministers of these churches often tell people to pray about their problems rather than do something about them. These churches, according to the group, substitute worship and shouting for activism. The group's leader, Speech, creates a vivid image:

> Sitting in church hearing legitimate woes.
> Pastor tells the lady it'll be alright,
> Just pray so you can see the pearly gates so white.
> The lady prays and prays and prays and prays
> and prays and prays and prays and prays . . . it's
>   everlasting.
> "There's nothing wrong with prayin'?" it's what she's
>   asking.[14]

He continues by saying she should be praying for changed circumstances, but church doctrine suggests that she simply "cope" with present evils. Instead of concrete social transformation, too many, according to Speech, content themselves with emotional release through worship but shouting only makes them lose their voice. One can assume he means this loss of voice in both physiological and political terms.

The Challenge of Black Theology

In response to the Black Church's ambiguous or inconsistent relationship to black communities, a group of Black Church–based theologians suggested a more aggressive approach to the gospel of Christ and its implications for human life. These thinkers argued that God had a preferential option for the oppressed that made the suffering of black Americans unacceptable. In a radical move theologian James Cone argued that God was ontologically black and anyone who claimed the label of Christian had to also become ontologically black. By this he meant being Christian in the United States required a commitment to and full participation in the ending of oppression. In Cone's words:

> Those who want to know who God is and what God is doing must know who black persons are and what they are doing. This does not mean lending a helping hand to the poor and unfortunate blacks of society. It does not mean joining the war on poverty! Such acts are sin offerings that represent a white way of assuring themselves that they are basically "good" persons. Knowing God means being on the side of the oppressed, becoming one with them, and participating in the goal of liberation. We must become black with God![15]

This call to activism differed from that proposed by Martin Luther King, Jr., in that Cone and other black theologians, for example, expressed an openness to the possibility of violence. For them, King's response was myopic in that it failed to recognize the intimate relationship between violence and the development of the United States. They understood the United States had secured its freedom from Great Britain through arms and had dealt with every other crisis through armed struggle. Violence was already a reality in America. The concern, then, for black theology was the nature of violence: does it free the oppressed or further enslave them? Concerning this Cone writes:

> Violence already exists. The Christian does not decide between violence and nonviolence, evil and good. He decides between the lesser and the greater evil. He must ponder whether revolutionary violence is less or more deplorable than the violence perpetuated by the system. There are no absolute rules which can decide the answer with certainty. But he must make a choice.[16]

What one finds in this theological reasoning is a much more radical stance than the "ethic of love" advocated by black Christians involved in the civil rights movement. This ethic was based on an assumption that oppressors would willingly surrender power once the error of their ways was pointed out through nonviolent direct action. Love, as theologically explained by the civil rights movement's leadership, is not weak. It is not a surrender to powerful forces; rather, it is a corrective for harmful forces in that it promotes a courageous stand against oppression through protest that recognizes the value and importance of each human life. Martin L. King, Jr., and others believed Black Power to be a misdirection, a useless appeal to violence that could only breed more violence. In King's words:

> Beneath all the satisfaction of a gratifying slogan, Black Power was a nihilistic philosophy born out of the conviction that the Negro can't win. It was, at bottom, the view that American society is so hopelessly corrupt and enmeshed in evil that there is no possibility of salvation from within. Although this thinking is understandable as a response to a white power structure that never completely committed itself to true equality for the Negro, and a die-hard mentality that sought to shut all windows and doors against the winds of change, it nonetheless carried the seeds of its own doom. . . . I cannot make myself believe that God wanted me to hate. I'm tired of violence, I've seen too much of it. I've seen such hate on the faces of

too many sheriffs in the South. And I'm not going to let my oppressor dictate to me what method I must use. Our oppressors have used violence. Our oppressors have used hatred. Our oppressors have used rifles and guns. I'm not going to stoop down to their level.[17]

Black Power advocates did not see any concrete benefit to King's strategy. From their perspective this appeal to oppressors through love and moral suasion only meant black bodies beaten by white officials and mobs. Black theology made a call for black power as a mode of Christian conduct that ran contrary to King's perspective. This meant black Christians should no longer "turn the other cheek" when confronted with violence designed to maintain the status quo. The appeal to Jesus as a nonviolent redeemer no longer set the stage for the struggle for civil rights in the late twentieth century. According to James Cone:

Each situation has its own problematic circumstances which force the believer to think through each act of obedience without an absolute ethical guide from Jesus. To look for such a guide is to deny the freedom of the Christian man. His only point of reference is the freedom granted in Christ to be all for the neighbor. Therefore, simply to say that Jesus did not use violence is no evidence relevant to the condition of black people as they decide on what to do about white oppression.[18]

Black Christians struggling for the liberation of oppressed black America must determine their own means of resistance, and violence remains a live option. From the perspective of black theology, the proclaiming of this radical interpretation of the gospel was the theologian's role. According to Cone: "Black theologians must assume the dangerous responsibility of articulating the revolutionary mood of the black community. This means that their speech about God, in the authentic prophetic tradition, will always move on the brink of treason and heresy in an oppressive society."[19] This concern with human liberation from racism became the central premise of black theology. Black theologians like Cone challenged the Black Church to take part in this mission and once again become God's tool for liberation. In extending this call, black theologians made an effort to partner with black churches. Cone asks: "How can black churches renew themselves without a black theology of renewal? How can the churches read the signs of the time if there are no prophetic theologians who can distinguish truth from heresy?"[20]

Although some larger black churches make use of academic liberation theology as a theological basis for their agenda and activities, most black churches are not significantly influenced by academic discussions. As James Harris, pastor of Second Baptist Church in Richmond, Virginia, puts it:

> Few ministers and laypersons who labor in black churches are aware that black theology is a discipline of study and reflection. Consequently, interest in and understanding of black liberation theology barely exists among the majority of persons that I have encountered in the black church. While my contextual experience as pastor has been limited to a few thousand people, my colleagues in the practice of pastoral ministry corroborate this perception.[21]

Professional theologians recognized this gap. According to Cone:

> I still am not convinced that the major black denominational churches are ready for renewal, but I do believe that there were and still are many genuinely committed black pastors and lay persons who transcend the limitations of their denominational identity by becoming identified with Christ through a commitment to the poor. They are found in all denominations (black as well as white) and they seemed determined to build more humane church structures that serve the community.[22]

Even with this being the case, according to Cone, "when black theology sought to return to the church of its origin in the late 1970s, it found that its absence had created an alienation and that black church leaders were not open to criticisms coming from professional theologians teaching in white institutions."[23]

The Charge of Anti-Intellectualism

Cone's statement points to an anti-intellectualism within the contemporary Black Church that makes critical engagement of the Church's history and thought somewhat problematic. In all fairness, there have been points during recent years when black theology and the Black Church were in fruitful dialogue. For example, during the mid-1970s the National Committee of Black Churchmen (NCBC) drafted another statement on black theology geared toward a church-based readership. In addition, the Black Theology Project first held in 1977 served as an opportunity to bring the Church and Academy together. Notwithstanding these events, a gap remained. The distance between many professional scholars of black religion and the Black Church continued to grow as these scholars pushed a liberal agenda that many churches objected to. (For example, many of these scholars have targeted homophobia within black churches; there will be more on this in chapter 5.) Theologian Renée L. Hill provides one of the more challenging critiques:

> Christianity has been on many occasions if not simply inadequate, downright destructive. As a black lesbian I wrestle mightily with a Christian religious heritage that has had its share of supporting and promoting misogyny, white supremacy, and the hatred of homosexuals. For too many people, the Christian message has not been a message of liberation. The Bible has been used as a weapon to enslave Africans, silence women, and abuse lesbians and gay men. Racists and misogynists have hidden behind church tradition to justify their destructive policies and actions. The black theology that was taking shape thirty years ago certainly recognized this fact in its recasting of Christianity as black power itself.[24]

In making such a strong critique, certain forms of black theology distanced themselves from the rather conservative posture of most black churches. And churches, in turn, insulated themselves from more liberal theological positions coming from the "ivory tower."

Troubled by what appeared to be a widening gap and growing hostility between professional black theology and black churches, some theologians articulated an apologetic for their work that sought to highlight inherent points of agreement and shared history between the aims of black theology and the Black Church. The general challenge was to address black theology on the local level, within particular churches, as a way of enhancing ministry through a critical engagement of faith. In this sense black theology can be a pastoral aid, a tool by which ministers can continue the critique of social injustice while developing progressive agendas and programs. Furthermore, ensuring a successful bridging of this gap is dependent on academics recognizing the importance for church members of practice or the doing of faith over against theory. And the Black Church must recognize the manner in which critical engagement of faith can result in a stronger and clearer understanding and commitment to the spirit of one's faith. This is happening within some local settings. For example, Samuel Berry McKinney, pastor of Mt. Zion Baptist Church of Seattle, and J. Alfred Smith, Sr., of Allen Temple Baptist Church make use of black theological principles and insights to enhance their ministry. In the words of Smith:

Both of these churches are engaged in linking black theology to black church history, through stained glass windows that articulate the message of women and men pioneers in the radical and revolutionary history of the African American legacy. Moreover, both churches have linked theological praxis to the global struggle of the Third World and actively support the liberating activity of the gospel in Africa. Black power and black theology, within the curriculum content of Sunday church school literature, could provide liberation and healing for the competitive, contentious, and conflicting role of gender relationships between black men and black women. . . . On the parish level, an application of black theology and black power in the area of stewardship of money would empower African American communities."[25]

Islam: The Challenge of Religious Diversity

From the antebellum period through the present, some who struggled economically, politically, and culturally and found little help in the Black Church turned to alternate religious orientations such as Judaism, African-based traditions, Islam, and others. One of the more widely discussed is the Nation of Islam, which appealed to many because of its strong critique of white society and because it placed blacks on the level of gods, although it provided no more in the way of social activism than did the Black Church. Sonsyrea Tate's story provides a glimpse into the appeal of the Nation of Islam for many black Americans. Tate was born into a family three generations deep into the Nation, all committed to the teachings of the Honorable Elijah Muhammad:

> "Elijah Muhammad told the people what they needed to hear at the time," my grandmother told me. "They needed somebody to make them feel good about themselves. Somebody to tell them yes, they were good. Whereby the white man had treated us so bad and made us out to be the bad ones. Well, the Honorable Elijah Muhammad came along and did the reverse." . . . My family was among tens of thousands who joined the Nation of Islam in search of a better way. In the Nation of Islam, we had our own identity and our own ethics. We had our own constitution, our own businesses, our own educational system—not just schools, but our own system and our own way of life.[26]

What Tate and her grandmother speak to is a sense of order, discipline, and history that helped many black Americans make sense of the world when other black-run organizations, including the Black Church, held a less firm sense of black consciousness and black nationalism.

While the Honorable Elijah Muhammad addressed perceived short-comings in black Christianity through the Nation of Islam, his son, Warith Deen Muhammad, represents a move by many black Americans into the world community of Islam through the Muslim American Society. Others have left black churches and simply identify themselves as Sunni Muslims. An example is the Dar-ul-Islam community begun in Brooklyn during the 1960s. In fact, according to scholar of Islam Jane Smith, "by the time of Elijah Muhammad's death in 1975, the Dar claimed more than thirty mosque-based Sunni Muslim communities. At that point, before Warith Deen began to move former NOI members toward ortho-dox Islam, the Dar was the largest black Sunni Muslim organization in the country, with mosques as far west as Colorado and in the West Indies, Ontario, and Alaska."[27]

Black Islamic communities within the United States, combined with the perpetual presence of African-based religious traditions such as voo-doo and others made it difficult for black churches to see themselves as the "only game in town." Neither the presence of mosques, synagogues, voodoo temples, and so forth, nor the statistics indicating rapid growth in the number of black muslims, for example, could be ignored. An exclusive link to or rhythm with the religious urges of black Americans did not exist for the Black Church. Reluctantly, it had to acknowledge the longstanding religious diversity of black communities and find its place (and purpose) within a religiously complex environment.

The Failed American Dream and Church Growth—1990s

The Middle Class and Changing Church Demographics

Although the impact of the Nation of Islam and other religious com-munities, as well as the other challenges noted above, has been notewor-thy, it is unwise to think of the past three decades as marking the Black Church's nadir. In fact, some scholars argue that rather than an overall trend toward Black Church decline, it is more likely that some indi-vidual churches declined while others have experienced tremendous growth. C. Eric Lincoln and Lawrence Mamiya, using statistics for 1987, state that roughly "78 percent of the black population claimed church membership and attended once in the last six months; blacks (44 per-cent) tend to have slightly higher rates of weekly church attendance than white Protestants (40 percent); and they have the highest rates of being superchurched (attending church more than once a week) among all Americans."[28] Sociologically viable examples of Lincoln's and Mamiya's findings would have to include Free At Last Church of God in Christ located in Minneapolis, pastored by Rev. Joseph Webb. It has relocated several times during its history in order to accommodate increased membership. Beginning with thirty members in 1985, it had by 1993 grown to fifteen hundred, with an average age of thirty.[29] Such impressive growth raises a question: what facilitated it? One gets a sense of how this question might be answered from one of the members, Clarissa Wells, who says: "The spirit of God is in this place. . . . It's so real. It's different from anything I've encountered before. I can feel the love in here."[30]

Free At Last Church of God in Christ and others like it make it difficult to accept a general hypothesis of church decline during the past three decades. No doubt some have left black churches because their material comforts, such as good homes and fine cars, have made the Church as a means of socioeconomic opportunity irrelevant, and others have left because of continuing crises seemingly ignored by the Church. But the success of the middle class and the troubles of the working class actually have played a dual role, driving some people back to the Church.[31] The black middle class expressed a feeling of living between two worlds, one generated by economic success and the other premised upon racial classification. As philosopher Cornel West points out, after the civil rights movement many members of the black elite maintained at least a rhetorical connection to the struggle for black advancement, but much of this was really self-serving. As of the late 1960s "the message was clear: beneath the rhetoric of Black Power, black control and black self-determination was a budding, 'New,' black, middle class hungry for power and starving for status."[32] Class and race, among other factors, now served to divide the black community into a relative small group of upwardly mobile and well-off blacks and a struggling majority population. Yet despite gains, middle-class blacks found themselves in search of a stabilizing force, a community. For those who followed their dreams out of cities, life in the suburbs proved troubling; racial discrimination could make property difficult to secure and, even when housing was found, fires and other forms of violence were often used to protest their presence:

> In recent years [this was written in 1984], a black college teacher's home in Chicago was fire bombed and vandalized; crosses were burned at black suburban homes around the country; rocks were thrown through windows and arson was attempted at a black home

in Cleveland Heights; a vacant home was burned in New Jersey when rumors were spread that a black family had bought it.[33]

Accompanying these difficulties was a cultural uncertainty, a shaky and often changing meaning of what it was to be "black." Many middle-class black Americans found themselves "outside the loop," considered foreigners by both less well-off blacks and whites. To combat this, many returned to their religious roots. In the words of journalist Beverly Hall Lawrence:

> As we mature, many of us now are looking back to what seems like "the good old days," to those traditional institutions like churches in hopes of finding guidance and a framework for living. Now that we're nearing middle age and are raising families, boomers are beginning to contemplate the meaning of life. We are returning, therefore, in part, because religion can provide a framework for basic questions regarding the origin, purpose, and meaning of life. Passage into middle age and the new spirituality, therefore, account for some of this revival of interest by blacks, but there are also indications that many are returning to the church in hopes of reviving its role as a command center and strategic outpost in our community.[34]

Churches have been more than pleased to welcome these religious seekers. Rev. Fred A. Lucas, former pastor of Bridge Street AME Church in New York, speaks about the new presence of professional blacks in glowing terms:

> We are blessed in the pew with a new generation of young black professionals who want to invest something in the resurrection of the black community. Many of them are relocating from the suburbs where their mamas and daddies and grandparents fled from the inner city. And they're coming back to be close to their jobs; they're tired of commuting the long distances. And they want to be in historic black communities. And they are affiliating with historic black denominations and churches.[35]

In other words, "across the country, there is a discernible turn back to the Church among educated, affluent blacks. As a young man, Baltimore civil engineer Larry Little, 41, forsook religion for radical politics. Years later, he felt isolated as the only black in his Ph.D. program at

Johns Hopkins and resumed churchgoing, currently at Baltimore's Bethel AME Church."[36] Another member of Bethel, Sandra Harley Adams, described this development in a way many members of the black middle class might appreciate:

> I think a lot of people our age, the reason why we're coming back is that we've had trauma in our lives. We've had bad marriages, we've had bad careers, and, personally, it was a relational thing for me. I thought for a long time I was master of my universe, but then you find you need something real. Something authentic through the church, through your own personal relationship with God.[37]

Benefits of Communal Leadership and a Renewed Public Presence

Although welcomed, the presence of parishioners such as Larry Little and Sandra Adams posed a challenge to traditional notions of church leadership. In the eighteenth and nineteenth centuries black clergy were arguably the best educated group in the black community. However, growth in educational opportunities during the post–civil rights movement years meant many congregants were better educated than their pastors, and this raised questions concerning traditional church hierarchies. Highly trained professionals within the congregation made unrealistic the idea that the pastor is invariably the person best equipped to manage all aspects of the church's ministry. As a result, leadership as a congregational responsibility, drawing on the talents and strengths of each member, is a style of leadership more noticeable over the past three decades. Recent studies point to the significance of this lay leadership. According to Sidney Verba, "nearly 40 percent of African Americans practice organizing skills at their place of worship, compared to only 20 percent of Latinos and 28 percent of Anglo-whites."[38]

Increased attention to lay leadership is not the sole factor in the reevaluation of the minister's centrality and status. The conduct of ministers shown to have "feet of clay" has tarnished the reputation of the Black Church and its leadership. Prominent examples include the recent financial mismanagement of convention funds by former president of the National Baptist Convention, U.S.A., Inc., Rev. Henry Lyons, who is serving a jail sentence because of his actions. His financial misdeeds point out an undercurrent of materialism in many black churches that calls into question the motivation that guides black ministers. Lyons's behavior points to the need for churches to decrease their dependence on charismatic leadership and to rely on a more communal model of authority. In addition, the scandal involving Rev. Jesse Jackson, a Baptist minister, who recently admitted having a child through an adulterous relationship with an employee of his Rainbow PUSH Network, has tainted perceptions of ministry on both the national and local level. This is just one example of clergy sexual misconduct, a break in professional ethics, that troubles many churches.

Of course, ethical and moral dilemmas are not limited to national religious leadership. Ministers on the local level have also been guilty of misdeeds, including the type of sexual misconduct Jackson recently confessed, and the disillusionment it generates can be as damaging. In the words of an AME pastor:

> When ministers engage in sexual misconduct, it has a significant effect on the members of the congregation in the church in which the misconduct occurs. Even if the minister leaves the local church, the misconduct changes the way in which many parishioners understand both God and the church. It affects the ways in which members perceive ministers. The actions of offending clergy affect the spirituality of the members, the role of the church in the community and the future of the local church after the misconduct has been revealed.[39]

The distress to which this minister points presents a valuable lesson. Those who depend too heavily on the charismatic leadership of a pastor find it difficult to overcome such a person's lapses in judgment. Because the church's vision is controlled by this one person, his or her failure is assumed to point to the failure of the proposed agenda. Furthermore, as Cornel West points out, charismatic leadership is usually developed at the expense of grassroots organizing. It tends to reduce "people's participatory possibilities—at the level of followership and leadership."[40]

Black churches survive and thrive, however, when this model of charismatic leadership is replaced by a model of collective leadership. Politicians and other community leaders, for instance, recognize the potential of black churches to shape opinions of those living in urban areas. The expertise of professionals participating in inner-city churches often results in political parties and candidates seeking their assistance. For example, Abyssinian Baptist Church in New York City printed the following in a 1993 bulletin: "Manhattan Borough President Ruth Messinger is seeking a number of organizers to join her grassroots reelection campaign. The ability to work with a wide range of people, personal organization and commitment to progressive politics are among the qualities they are looking for, and a sense of humor wouldn't hurt. Specific requirements are listed with each job description."[41] This is more than just a job advertisement, because it points to a recognition of the Black Church's potential for political activism and voting strength evidenced in the late twentieth century. Winning votes and developing successful programs in inner-city communities require attention to black churches because of the attention given to political issues by black Christians. According to a 1984 *USA Today* poll, "blacks were three times more likely (28 percent) than whites (8 percent) to report that their religious leaders discussed politics all the time or frequently. They were also more likely than whites (31 percent compared to 21 percent) to report that such discussions took place 'sometimes.'"[42]

"Generation X" and the Church

Increased involvement of churches in pressing political issues during the 1990s brought the work of the Black Church to the attention of many who held no prior knowledge of the Church. While the influx of these "first timers" bolstered the potential for the local church's activism, it also forced an evaluation of inner workings of the Black Church. For example, churches had to make fewer assumptions concerning acquaintance with traditional church etiquette (proper dress and conduct) and concerning familiarity with church ritual and doctrine.[43] Alteration to expectations also required a sensitivity to the needs of young people attracted to the revived political face of the Church. Creative youth programs, using Afrocentrism, have been vital for churches seeking to attract and maintain the membership of young people. In essence, Afrocentrism is a viewing of history, cultural, and social developments from the perspective of those of African descent. Within the contemporary Church, the presentation of this philosophy usually takes the form of rites of passage that connect African ritual sensibilities and contemporary black American cultural needs. The object is to promote a sense of connection to community through principles of responsibility, respect, cooperation, perseverance, and service. These principles are part of a larger concern with instilling an appreciation for worship, prayer, and faith. All this is framed by an understanding of African and black American history. For young men, these principles and corresponding history are communicated by older men, and for young girls, older women serve as guides. This is because older members of the community—elders— are the bearers of cultural information and therefore are key to the proper communication of cultural values. According to Barbara Eklof, those who receive and act on this information are recognized as new adults through an elaborate ceremony that celebrates "the positive aspects of moving from childhood to adulthood; exalting our ancestral traditions;

instilling a sense of values in the initiates while glorifying their physical, emotional, mental, spiritual uniqueness."[44] A representative ceremony for young men is outlined by theologian J. Deotis Roberts:

> The male honoree lies face down on the floor before his parents. The mother says, "Arise, precious fruit of my womb and take my blessing." The honoree rises. The mother offers the first half of the anointing prayer, and the father completes it. Then the anointing begins. First, the father dips his thumb in the blessed oil or ointment and makes a triangle on his son's forehead. Then the mother dips her thumb in the same oil or ointment and makes a circle around the triangle. [He] is then spiritually anointed. The ceremony is concluded by an elder, minister, or priest by these words: "Arise, precious fruit of our people and take my blessing."[45]

Such practices have proven useful and have resulted, in many cases, in an embrace of the Church and its teachings as the Church demonstrates its concern with and respect for young people.

Much of the attention, however, given to young people centers on the rescue of young men and the promotion of masculinity as a core feature of the Black Church. In part this move is inspired by the tragic statistics related to young black males in the late twentieth century. For example, during the past few decades the number of black males in the prison system (or awaiting sentencing) has soared, while their enrollment in higher education has declined. In recent years the life expectancy of black males in many major urban centers has declined to under fifty years. One easily sees why churches would turn their attention to the rescue of young black males, but this approach is often myopic and problematic. (The potential problems behind this approach are addressed in chapter 6, but at this point attention is simply given to it as a form of ministry.)

According to researcher and AME Church member Herbert H. Toler, Jr.:

> Men who visit Bethel [Church in Baltimore] also find an atmosphere that is masculine as well as feminine, unlike many of the churches they are used to. At age 13 or so, many black youths tend to drop out of church. At that age, black males who were once drawn to the choir as youth no longer sing, because robes look like dresses. Their Sunday school teachers, superintendents, and youth advisers are women. Their reaction to the religious femininity of the church drives them out of the church and into the seduction of a gang.[46]

To counter this, Bethel Church and others like it provide mentors for young men to teach them modes of proper conduct and the important role the church can play in their lives. In addition to church activities such as rites of passage and Bible studies, Bethel Church also models responsibility to young people as a form of ministry. For example:

> After a small riot erupted at Booker T. Washington Junior High School just before Christmas last year [1994], Bethel began a direct partnership with the school. To prevent a reoccurrence, [Pastor Frank] Reid summoned 150 men to the school. They lined the street in front of the school and remained watchful for arsonists, gangs and visiting troublemakers. At the request of the principal, the men recently returned to supervise the children in the morning and afternoon. The pupils' tranquility prompted one teacher to comment that they were "acting like children again."[47]

1970s–1990s: Growth and Decline?

The above discussion, in which both the decline and growth of black churches are presented as the major markers of the late twentieth century, may seem a bit odd, but it is accurate. First, the economic, social, and political developments of the 1970s and 1980s created through the struggles of the 1960s produced a middle class with new advantages and professional status. In many cases members of this class considered themselves far better equipped to address their needs than the pastor of a church. Their success, according to many, made the Church and what it could offer unnecessary and at times burdensome. This resulted in an awkwardness between the Black Church and this prosperous component of black America. For some, the Black Church had succeeded in securing the advance of black Americans and had in the process rendered itself irrelevant with respect to socioeconomic and political life. And the spirituality it pushed seemed easily replaced with a return to African sensibilities, Islam, or any number of New Age religious developments growing out of a fascination with the East. In addition, the Black Church and its optimism and self-assurance had been radically damaged by the killing of Martin Luther King, Jr. Leadership in black America had revolved around religious leaders for the most part, and this "Moses" for the twentieth century had been cut down by a bullet. This created a void in leadership that fostered a crisis of vision and purpose. In this sense the 1970s marked a period of transition for both religious community and the larger black communities that would extend through the 1980s. The effects of this disillusionment and resulting transition were far-reaching; children born during these two decades spent little time in the Church and looked elsewhere for success. The Black Church's generally lax attitude concerning socioeconomic and political developments after its civil rights activities did not help young people wrestling with crack cocaine and the problems it generated during the 1980s. One finds a youthful response to the Church in particular and society in general in the rap music produced during the 1980s and the early 1990s, all developed by young people born during the decades of decline.

Many members of the black middle class assumed that their material success would open doors and allow them full inclusion in American society. During the 1990s they realized this was not the case, and old institutions that had once provided cultural and social stability became important again. The Church took on new meaning for the black middle class and the children growing up within these families, resulting in church growth. By 1997 the Black Church claimed over 25 million members in more than 63,000 congregations.[48]

Burnings! A Late-Twentieth-Century Challenge to the Church

After the years of church bombings during the civil rights struggle, the hate crime of church burnings arose. One of the most graphic was the attacks on St. John Baptist Church of South Carolina:

> In 1983, while Sunday services were underway, a group of whites shot out the church's windows. Coming back later in the day, they scrawled "KKK" on the door, destroyed the piano, smashed the crucifix, tore up the Bibles, scattered beer cans on the pews, and even defecated on the sacrament cloth. Over the next 12 years, more than 200 people were arrested for acts of vandalism against the church. Then, on August 15, 1995, the church was burned down.[49]

Church burnings during the 1990s centered in Pike and Amite counties in Mississippi, which, during the 1960s, were often referred to as the "church burning capitals of the world," with some twenty in a decade. Records indicate that burnings in Pike and Amite are part of a larger trend, with ninety burnings reported between 1990 and 1996 in Mississippi, Tennessee, Alabama, South Carolina, and Louisiana.[50]

Although not all of the churches burned were black, nor were all cases ruled arson or committed by whites, the vast majority were small black churches in rural areas with the crimes committed by white males between the ages of 14 and 45.[51] It is likely that the small size of these congregations translated into little sociopolitical authority and limited visibility, and this meant practically no media and federal attention until 1995. But even media attention and governmental investigation (using some two hundred federal agents by 1996, the operation, known as the Church Arson Task Force, involved both the Justice Department and the Treasury) proved frustrating for many churches and activists because the factor of racism was downplayed. According to Ron Nixon and Dennis Bernstein: "Whenever it comes to attacks on black people, those who attack us are always given the benefit of the doubt. . . . In many of these cases, they have no idea who's burning these churches. How do they know it's not racism if they are not looking? So far, law enforcement has refused to call these burnings what they are: racist acts of terrorism."[52] Beyond debate over charges of racism *vs.* more generic explanations for the burnings, the destruction of these churches made a statement. It pointed to the continued understanding of the Black Church as a major nerve center for black life. Talking about the South in particular, Pamela Berry's statement is applicable across geographic lines: "Anybody in the South knows that the strength of the black community is our churches. When they start to burn our churches, they're trying to take away our strength."[53]

Many of those who entered black churches for the first time during the past three decades and others who returned from a long absence did so in the hope that the Black Church would prove itself the black community's strength. While this appeal to the Church's socioeconomic and political potential has been important, many also point to the value of worship as well. For them, the vibrancy of the Church is tied to the experience of worship that frames activism by building a strong sense of self—the individual in connection to community and God.

3

Beliefs and Worship
in the Black Church

What the Church Believes

What doctrine has shaped the development and activism of the Black Church? What are the elements of faith held across denominational lines that give the Black Church its character and sanction its activities? How are these beliefs acted out within the local church setting? These questions point to the body of beliefs and ritual practices that undergird the institutional Black Church and provide the parameters for what it means to be black and Christian for roughly 24 million black Americans.

Black Christians do not hold all elements of doctrine or belief in common. Yet there are many points of doctrinal and ritual agreement that unite the thousands of congregations across the country. It is these doctrinal and ritual elements that define the black Christian tradition. This is not to say that all black Christians give the same importance to each element or that every black Christian has even given serious consideration to the merits of this accepted doctrine. In some cases black Christians confess its importance, but their daily lives do not mirror the responsibilities it generates. For example, many black Christians speak about the scriptural requirement to tithe (give 10 percent of one's income) but still fail to share their economic resources with their church. Others are less vocal about the centrality of church doctrine to daily activities but demonstrate this commitment to the basic elements of faith through their dealings with others. For instance, some may never read their denomination's official doctrine and polity to find requirements regarding charity, but they give time to community-service projects because they think it's the right thing to do. Regardless of inconsistencies within the lives of believers, the doctrine presented here is important and central because it represents a historically significant and commonly accepted thread of meaning within the Black Church Tradition. This chapter presents several basic beliefs (related to the Trinity, human nature, salvation, and the Bible) and practices (worship through music, sermons, testimonies, and prayer) that have shaped the Black Church from its years as the invisible institution to its contemporary incarnation.

God with Us—The Trinity

From the period of slavery to the present, black Christians have devoted themselves to a God who is believed to be present in the world. The idea of a God distant from the world and unconcerned with human affairs never appealed to black Christians, whose existential situation seemed to require superhuman effort to correct. Within the invisible institution and in contemporary churches, black Christians talk about God as loving, kind, just, compassionate, and defined by a demand for justice and righteousness. These characteristics and attributes are placed in context by drawing on scriptural stories of God's encounters with other oppressed communities. Black Christians assume that God's work extended through all times to all suffering peoples, including them. Norman W. Brown articulates this understanding of God in a way that is representative of the general belief:

> My mother's God was the God who fed her fatherless children, and would fight her battles and subdue her enemies. As adequate as that may be, it is but a shadow of a more complete revelation of God, whose immutable laws binds a million words to the seat of universal government; watches the tiny ant as it ploughs the trackless desert. Takes cognizance of the sparrow that falls and numbers every hair of your head, and bottles up your tears.[1]

This connection between God and suffering humanity was viewed as being so strong that it shaped the very being of God. Bishop Henry McNeal Turner of the AME Church expressed this ontological character of God in a 1895 speech given in Altanta, in which he argued that "God is a Negro." James Cone has continued this line of reasoning by claiming that "the blackness of God means that God has made the oppressed condition God's own condition. This is the essence of the biblical revelation."[2]

Whereas black Christians are in agreement on the nature of God and God's role in the world, there remains a debate over gender-neutral language. Many ministers still refer to God as "he," and many church members also use this language because it is the traditional way to refer to God. Young men and women who have entered ministry within the past several decades, however, tend to reject gender-specific God language, and they encourage their congregations also to avoid this language. Referring to God in ways that reflect both male and female (for example, God as Parent as opposed to God the Father) speaks to an effort on the part of many to connect God to the entire black community.

The relationship between the divine and human life is further developed through a basic belief in Jesus Christ, the second component of the Trinity, as present in and with the contemporary Christian community. In keeping with the scriptural account of Jesus Christ, black Christians believe that Jesus Christ redeemed humanity from its original sin through his death on the cross and resurrection from the dead. This death-resurrection event is remembered within the Church through Sunday communion—consumption of bread and wine (or grape juice) representing the body and blood of Jesus sacrificed on the cross. The Black Church teaches that those who recognize that God sent Jesus to save the world from its sin and accept him as their personal savior have Jesus in their hearts. The Church of God in Christ, for example, phrases it this way: "We believe that the redemptive work of Christ on the Cross provides healing for the human body in answer to believing in prayer."[3] Beyond the condition of the individual soul, this relationship with Christ is believed to have importance with respect to daily existence. As a young woman who joined a Methodist Church in 1984 stated: "I think when you're black, when you're in pain, there are three things that you call upon: your mother, your father, and Jesus Christ."[4]

Black Christians generally believe in a second coming of Christ, when Jesus will return to judge the world, punish sinners, and reward the redeemed. For example, regarding this, the National Baptist Convention, U.S.A., Inc., states that "those who believe in Christ at the second coming will ascend to heaven (a state of paradise) to reside with the holy trinity. The dead believers will likewise be raised from the dead and 'reborn' with perfect, new bodies in heaven. Those who do not believe in Christ will be relegated to a place of endless punishment."[5] A Methodist minister phrased it this way: "The trumpet sound that the Bible speaks about will be heard and the sea will give up its dead and the graves will open. Those that are alive will be caught up with Jesus Christ in the sky and will go to heaven."[6]

Whereas Jesus Christ brought salvation to humanity, the Holy Spirit, the third Person within the Trinity, makes available spiritual gifts and talents that help the faithful live a richer life. Drawing from the Bible, black Christians argue that when Christ arose from the dead and ascended into heaven he promised the Holy Spirit "for the purpose of equipping and empowering the believer, making him a more effective witness for service in the world."[7] There is general agreement concerning the availability of the Holy Spirit to believers. Of more controversy, however, is the sign of this presence. With respect to this, only the Church of God in Christ gives priority to speaking in tongues as *the* sign of the Holy Spirit. The other denominations argue that this is certainly one of the signs but not the only sign. Therefore, Christians can have the Holy Spirit within them and this can be manifest through a process as simple as having asked God for the Holy Spirit in their lives and then having experienced emotions (for example, joy or peace) that convince them the request was granted. Furthermore, black Christians across the various denominations in varying degrees believe that the presence of the Holy Spirit can also be marked by dancing in the spirit and shouting. Although most strongly held by the Church of God in Christ, black Christians in the other denominations do acknowledge as possibilities the ability to heal or prophesy as consequences of the Holy Spirit's presence. This perspective is based on scriptural references such as the following: "And it shall come to pass in the last days, saith God, I will pour out of my Spirit upon all flesh: and your sons and your daughters shall prophesy, and your young men shall see visions, and your old men shall dream dreams" (Acts 2:17).

According to many, this interest in the Holy Spirit as an important component of spiritual growth penetrates Baptist and Methodist churches through what is commonly called the Neo-Pentecostal movement. Beginning in the 1970s this development, also referred to as the charismatic movement, entailed a call to deeper spirituality expressed in part through increased church involvement. According to historians C. Eric Lincoln and Lawrence Mamiya, "the lay members of these churches tend to be intensely involved with church activity on a daily basis, from prayer meetings and Bible study to adult education classes." Lincoln and Mamiya point out that with respect to church services "the charismatic style of worship is much more emotionally oriented."[8]

Humanity and Its Sinfulness

Members of the Black Church acknowledge human beings were created by God and reflect in their being the likeness of God. In the words of Genesis 1:26: "And God said, Let us make man in our image, after our likeness." This understanding of human nature means all humans have value and any attempt to degrade a human is contrary to the will of God. Furthermore, humans were created with free will, the ability to embrace or reject God's will. This entails a consciousness of good and evil *and* the ability to choose between them. Put another way, ethicist Peter Paris argues:

> The moral dimension of life comprises one of the most distinctive differences between human beings and other animals. Morality is expressive of the capacity to determine the quality of human activity by making choices in accordance with understandings of good and bad, right and wrong. As moral agents, human beings are able to perceive others as subjects, and in their encounter with them they may choose to treat them either as subjects or as objects.[9]

This is not a unique position. Very few Christians of any denomination would deny that humans were created in the image of God, with the ability to make choices. For black Christians, however, this has been intimately connected to the struggle for equality in human society. The belief that humans are not mere animals, based on the Genesis account of creation, has served as an argument against racist efforts to belittle blacks beginning with the period of slavery. It also provided a biblically based demand for treatment as subjects and not objects that framed civil rights activities of the 1960s.

Shortly after their creation, humans disobeyed God. Consequently, human nature is marked by a sinfulness that is passed on to each child. Humans, black Christians believe, sin on both the personal and the communal level. With respect to the former, acts of disobedience to God's will can take place through thought, word, or deed. Examples include covetous thoughts, lies, and theft. In more religiously rigid settings activities such as the use of tobacco, alcohol consumption, dancing, and swearing would also be included in a list of personal sins. These sins, according to the Black Church, are not to be ignored, but their ramifications in most cases only extend to a small group. Of more far-reaching consequence are communal sins such as racism, which affect entire communities. From the perspective of black Christians, the treatment black Americans have received throughout their history in North America is a matter of sin, misconduct tied to flawed human nature. This, however, does not excuse the conduct. It does not mean that this sin is unavoidable, hence beyond human accountability. Humans are responsible for their sins and, if repentance is not made, both personal and communal sins result in punishment from God.

Salvation and Black Experience

According to the Black Church, humans can be held accountable for their sins because they act in accordance with free will and because God offers salvation and forgiveness for past sins to anyone who asks for it. As noted above, the Black Church believes God sent Jesus Christ to suffer death on the cross in order to pay for humanity's sins. Securing salvation, or reconnection to God and God's will, entails several steps: (1) recognition of one's sinfulness and need for salvation; (2) belief that God sent Jesus Christ to redeem the world and offer redemption; (3) a heartfelt petition for God's forgiveness; and (4) belief that God has provided redemption in accordance with one's sincere petition. Once these steps are taken, a person is "born again," or freed from past sins and "born" into a new life within the community of believers. This process is a gift from God that cannot be purchased or earned. Rather, it is secured through faith and the grace of God. For black Christians, this process is summed up in scripture: "If thou shalt confess with thy mouth the Lord Jesus, and shalt believe in thine heart that God hath raised him from the dead, thou shalt be saved. For with the heart man believeth unto righteousness; and with the mouth confession is made unto salvation" (Rom 10:9-10). Redemption from sin and a new relationship with God that mark salvation are given symbolic expression through baptism. Whereas there is no consensus on the proper form of this baptism (for example, full immersion in water or sprinkling with water) there is general agreement on the meaning of baptism. Across denominational lines it represents the death of old human nature and the rebirth of the person in a life with God.

Acceptance of Jesus Christ as one's personal savior is the real test to determine those who are Christian. Many belong to the Church, and this makes them members of the Church, but it does not make them Christians. As George McKinney, pastor of St. Stephen's Church of God in Christ, says, "One of the tragedies of our day is that a large percentage of the members in the churches do not represent Jesus Christ properly. They attend church every Sunday; they worship, sing in the choir, take communion, give money, work in the church clubs, serve in various office capacities in the church, but as far as spirituality and real dedication are concerned, they are sadly lacking. . . . They live with no real evidence of a born-again experience."[10] Within the Black Church, salvation is linked to new conduct, and this conduct has consequences with respect to activism. In other words, black Christians argue that people "are saved to serve." Regeneration from sin provides a new outlook on life and a need both to spread the word of God's love and to change the oppressive situation under which the oppressed live. The ministers involved in the Kelly Miller Smith Institute on African-American Church Studies at Vanderbilt University Divinity School speak to this complex mission: "Across the United States today hundreds, perhaps thousands, of African-American congregations are demonstrating that it is possible to integrate their Blackness and their faith in a way that not only bestows wholeness and healing upon individuals and families, but also engages communities in corporate ministries of intervention and transformation of the structures of social, economic, and political life."[11]

Scripture and Interpretation

First during the period of slavery, as Africans gathered what they could from the Bible, through the late twentieth century, scripture has played an important role in the development of the Black Church's doctrine. Concerning this, historian Albert Raboteau writes, "the biblical orientation of slave religion was one of its central characteristics." Raboteau continues, saying that although most enslaved Africans could not read, "illiteracy proved less of an obstacle to knowledge of the Bible than might be thought, for biblical stories became part of the oral tradition of slaves. Oral instructions and Sunday School lessons were committed to memory."[12] Educational opportunities generated during the late nineteenth century by schools for blacks only increased reliance on scripture to define religious identities and secular responsibilities. The twentieth century is marked by a similar concern with scripture as a blueprint for proper living. Drawing from the various life questions and problems found in the Bible, members of the Black Church construct ethics and morals for daily life. For example, many black Christians use the Good Samaritan story told by Jesus as the rationale for helping those in need. Furthermore, the activities of biblical figures provide the rationale for activism for the Black Church. A prime example of this is presented by Martin Luther King, Jr., in explaining the spread of the struggle for civil rights by reference to the spread of God's message through biblical prophets and apostles:

> I am in Birmingham because injustice is here. Just as the prophets of the eighth century B.C. left their villages and carried their "thus saith the Lord" far beyond the boundaries of their hometowns, and just as the Apostle Paul left his village of Tarsus and carried the

gospel of Jesus Christ to the far corners of the Greco-Roman world, so am I compelled to carry the gospel of freedom beyond my own hometown. Like Paul, I must constantly respond to the Macedonian call for aid.[13]

As George McKinney notes, when Christians fail to live in accordance with scripture, problems ensue. "The church has too often lost the Biblical vision as to the purpose of the church. . . . The church has drifted far from the divine pattern and program as set forth in the Scriptures. Loss of vision and estrangement from God account for the spiritual declension in many of our churches today."[14]

Scripture holds this position because it is considered the inspired word of God, recorded by humans; it presents God's self-revelation and God's will for humankind. In this respect it differs from books written by denominations to outline beliefs because it serves as the unchanging basis for church doctrine. For some, this means the Bible should be taken literally as the infallible and inerrant word of God. That is to say, although it is physically recorded by fallible humans, God is in control of the process, and as a result the Bible is recorded without error and without being tainted by human desires and wants. This entails a conservative interpretation of scripture that provides little room for thinking about the meaning of scripture's lessons in light of the contemporary context. Other black Christians address scripture as the inspired word of God, but they argue that it must be placed in its historical-cultural context. That is to say, scripture must be read and interpreted with modern eyes and in light of socially constructed power dynamics. In other words, this more critical interpretation of scripture is premised upon the desire of those in power to maintain their authority through any means necessary, including the manipulation of sacred texts. So, minority groups must treat interpretations of scripture by dominant groups with suspicion (a hermeneutic of suspicion). This was the thinking when slaves rejected biblical evidence justifying their enslavement, and it continues to be the case for many black Christians. Based on this more critical reading, it is argued that the Bible's ethical and moral lessons must be learned, but scripture's cultural sensibilities (for example, first-century thinking on gender and family) are not necessarily applicable now. A good example of this perspective, also discussed in chapter 6, is the debate over women's roles in church ministry as outlined in scripture.

Those who reject the ordination of women argue that scripture, particularly 1 Corinthians 11:3, gives men control over both social and religious realms by means of a clearly laid out hierarchy: "But I would have you know, that the head of every man is Christ; and the head of the woman is the man; and the head of Christ is God." On the other hand, those who take the historical-cultural context of scripture into consideration recognize the patriarchy that marked the world during biblical days. And they do not hold the patriarchy of biblical times as normative and essential to the biblical message. Rather, they argue reading scripture for its message to believers entails moving beyond the oppressive tendencies of humans and hearing the will of God that lives behind the words. According to biblical scholar Elisabeth Schüssler Fiorenza, "this means that despite the sexist context in which the experience of the early Christian communities was canonized, the material can be viewed another way."[15] Minister and ethicist Katie Cannon makes a similar point:

The utterances of the preacher must be examined in the situation in which they are produced and delivered to the hearers, that is, in terms of the preacher's and congregation's own experiences. Nothing prohibits us from asking questions about the role of social factors in shaping sermonic texts and what part the preacher's gender plays in selecting the kinds of biblical stories and sayings that she or he uses in preaching.[16]

What Schüssler Fiorenza and Cannon point to is a practice by which many black Christians distinguish the customs of the communities in which the Bible developed from scripture's underlying moral and ethical teachings.

Worship as Celebration of Belief

While weekday activities such as Bible studies, choir rehearsals, and prayer meetings may not attract large numbers of participants, it is understood that Sunday worship is the basic form of celebration within the context of the Christian community. Thus it serves as the basic measure of involvement in the life of the Church and the basic sources of spiritual renewal and encouragement for members of the Black Church. Furthermore, it is the primary communal forum for expressing thanks and gratitude to God for salvation, and it is believed that God is present and felt during this period of worship. There is, of course, variation in how worship is conducted. For example, in some churches people come dressed in their best clothing and in others casual attire is the norm. Sunday service in some churches is short, and in others it is three hours long. Some services are reserved, with little emotional expression, and others are energetic and loud. Some involve elaborate robes, candles, denominationally determined customs, and numerous officiants, while others are simple and involve spontaneous congregational participation. There are a variety of components to worship, including the reading of announcements related to weekday activities, reading of scripture and confessions of faith, communion, and the collection of money to meet the church's expenses. However, worship in the Black Church is primarily defined by music, preaching, testimonies, and prayer.

Music in Black Worship

The historical contexts for the development of the spirituals and gospel music are very different. Spirituals grew out of the experience of slavery and the covert religious practices of enslaved Africans, referred

to as the invisible institution. Gospel music is a post-emancipation development, a product of the twentieth century and the concerns of the
Great Migration. Yet whether forged in the private gatherings of slaves
or the institutional churches of the twentieth century, there are shared
thematic elements revolving around the elements of doctrine noted above.

The spirituals and gospel music announce that all humans are made
in the image of God; hence, all human life is important and of equal
concern to God. This, however, did not prevent the world from being an
extremely harsh place, full of misery and pain, existential hardship and
psychic stress. Within this context of suffering, it is not uncommon to
feel isolated. How could this not be the case in light of the physical labor
slavery entailed or the disenfranchisement that plagued blacks after slavery? But this was not always so. The earth at creation was vital and
vibrant, friendly and supportive of life, and the positive relationship to
nature often present in the music speaks to this. The opposite of this
earth's hardships is heaven's bliss, and this more perfect place receives
attention in the spirituals and gospel. It is presented as a place where
abused Christians are given their "due." Commitment to high moral
standards and ethical conduct on earth is recognized and rewarded in
heaven, which is often presented as a free space on this earth. In other
cases, it is more certain that heaven is a reference to a place beyond earth
where the weary can rest and commune with Jesus and their loved ones.
Discussion of earth and heaven begs the question of salvation. With some
of the music it is clear that salvation revolves around a conversion experience, a surrender to the will of God. It is a lonely process in that each
individual must make the journey from evil ways to righteousness alone.
In accordance with this perspective, it is clear that mere lip service to the
Christian faith and superficial allegiance to church services and Bible
studies would not result in salvation. These activities may give the appearance of a Christian life, but they do not entail a surrender of the
"old nature" for a rebirth into the ways of Christ. That is to say, going
through the motions does not point to a regeneration of the heart and a
repentance from past misdeeds. Accordingly, "Ev'rybody talkin' 'bout
Heab'n ain't goin' there."[17]

According to historian John Lovell, there are some forty-six categories of biblical persons, places, and events mentioned in the spirituals,
and these categories are carried over into gospel music.[18] Current biblical scholars might be surprised by the freedom with which black religious music brings historical and biblical figures into conversation with
their current plight. It would not be uncommon to have Moses present,
or Jesus present, as if the community of the enslaved is in direct communication with these figures. Continuity with respect to time was not the

major issue in developing stories in the spirituals. In the place of proper chronology, slaves gave attention to existential connections. In other words, it was possible to bring the Children of Israel from the Hebrew Bible into conversation with black Americans because both had a common experience of misery and undeserved suffering. Within many of these songs the singers connected themselves epistemologically and existentially to the Children of Israel discussed in the Old Testament. This linking through a shared knowledge and experience of suffering and pain did not end with commiseration of bad times. To the contrary, like the Children of Israel—who are, according to scripture, the chosen people of God—blacks recognized themselves as set apart by God.

God recognized what was happening and was committed to bringing blacks through this pain and suffering. Dwelling in slavery or continued discrimination might counter this claim for some, but for those singing the spirituals and gospel music it was understood that God sometimes allowed the chosen people to be refined by "fire" and prepared for a great destiny. In this way the claim to chosen status might have been blacks' way of countering manifest destiny arguments by which colonists and their descendants claimed they had been set apart to establish the kingdom of God on earth. Kinship was not simply with the Children of Israel. Spirituals and gospel music also present blacks as being related to Christ. He is often referred to as a brother or friend, one who understands and empathizes with the plight of slaves and their descendants because he too suffered at the hands of the unjust. Sent by God to suffer for the sins of humanity and thereby make grace and salvation available to humankind, Christ endured the cross. Enslaved Africans, in like manner, suffered the abuse of slave holders, who used their labor to enrich white society, and blacks continue to serve the interests of corporate America. In both cases the wicked are not given the last word. Rather, the righteousness of the suffering servants is rewarded: the reign of Christ at the right hand of God after his resurrection from the dead speaks to this, and black Christians await their redemption.

Some mistakenly argue that the spirituals and gospel are strictly otherworldly and unconcerned with mundane events. This is far too simplistic when one considers that proper moral conduct and ethical ways of being in the world are major concerns expressed in the lyrics of spirituals and gospel music. Although presented in subtle ways to prevent physical abuse from offended whites, both forms of religious music speak in creative ways about sin and the coming punishment of sinners. For instance, couched in mild language, spirituals made it clear that those who suffered injustice would be rewarded and oppressors would be damned. Scripture often provided the language for this prophecy. Again, drawing on chosen people imagery, it was not uncommon for spirituals to portray slaves as the Children of Israel fleeing Egypt and slave holders as Pharaoh and his army, who are killed in the Red Sea. For slave holders and other unrighteous people, death would be a horrific event that is merely a precursor to judgment and eternal punishment. However, for the righteous, death, often symbolically discussed as crossing over the River Jordan, is a transition to something better. This understanding of redemption was carried over from the spirituals into gospel music.

Who is this God in charge of meting out rewards and punishment? God discussed by enslaved Africans and their twentieth-century descendants is the God presented in both the Hebrew Bible and the New Testament. As such, God is understood as loving, kind, just, compassionate, omnipresent, and omnipotent. And these attributes must ultimately result in God requiring accountability from oppressors, because while slave holders are powerful, God is *all* powerful, the ultimate source of all things. Furthermore, God as presented in the spirituals is also personal; God is available to individuals and is concerned with each element of creation. Spirituals and gospel also tend to portray God in anthropomorphic ways that seem reasonable for a people struggling for self-understanding and self-worth. It only makes sense in light of this quest for subjectivity to understand what is best about the universe—God—as being related to oneself.

Spirituals

In most record stores one can move through the aisles and locate works by Antonín Dvořák, the composer from Bohemia, including Symphony No. 9 ("From the New World"). Not only was this symphony inspired by his visit to North America and his encounter with black American spirituals in 1892, but he also claimed that the spirituals were the "only genuine folk music in America upon which a national music could be developed."[19] Others came to the same conclusion. In more recent years concert halls across the globe have been held spellbound by Jessye Norman's and Kathleen Battle's singing of spirituals. In earlier years the singing of Marian Anderson had the same effect. Contempo rary groups such as Sounds of Blackness ("The Evolution of Black Music") have also paid tribute to this music, and the king of funk, George Clinton (of Parliament and Funkadelics fame) is profoundly influenced by this music. One need only listen to his rendition of "Swing Low, Sweet Chariot" to have a sense of the depth of its influence. It is clear that the spirituals have inspired the U.S. musical scene. In addition to this impact on musical cultural production, the spirituals speak volumes concerning the history of black churches and their worship.

We cannot say for certain when and where the spirituals developed, although several scholars, such as folklorist Lydia Parrish, argue that South Carolina was the place of origin. Others, however, argue that the place of origin is probably closer to the North, in Virginia.[20] This debate aside, it is evident that spirituals became a subject of study around the time of the Civil War, when whites began to write commentary and record the lyrics, rhythms, and movements associated with spirituals. And some time later the Fisk Jubilee Singers and the Hampton Institute Singers took this musical form, revised it, and presented it around the world. Whenever and wherever their origin, it is fairly clear from the testimony of former slaves that spirituals provided a way of wrestling with the existential angst and hardships forced on black bodies and spirits by the institution of slavery. Questions, concerns, predictions and complaints that could not be made directly to slave holders and overseers could be voiced to a more understanding and eternal presence—God. The deep symbolic value of their religious language often made it possible to move these songs from the secret hush arbors to the open fields and meetings. After all, slave holders enjoyed the singing of their slaves, because for them it meant slaves were content or even happy with their condition and surroundings.

Some argue that the preachers' words during sermons and communal prayers served as the basis for spirituals. It is also possible that the hardships of the day put together with religious sensibilities in the development of this music. What is less questionable is the spontaneous nature of this musical creation and the role it played in shaping the early religious experience and format of black Americans. During meetings of various forms, the sensibilities of their African cultural traditions (such as scales and rhythm), the current context, the musical sensibilities of Europe (hymns such as "Dr. Watts" songs as found in his *Hymns and Spiritual Songs*), biblical stories, folk wisdom, and other resources were blended into a unique musical expression. Drums were outlawed for fear of secret messages leading to rebellion, so Africans used their bodies—clapping and foot tapping—to keep time and monitor the flow of these songs.

The spiritual, then, is a complex, multilayered, and syncretic style of song shaped by religious and theological regulations.[21] Although religious in orientation, spirituals borrowed style and rhythm from secular songs. Singers felt free to mix and match materials from existing tunes and use this process to forge alternate versions as well as relatively new pieces, as long as the final product spoke to their relationship with God. Typically by individuals, these spirituals were maintained through consensus, because songs only persisted in a community's repertoire if they were approved and adopted by the community. There is an added and extremely important communal dimension to this music that extends beyond the development of a canon. Ranking and ordering of spirituals aside, this music was also communal in that its inner workings and double-talk were known only to Africans. That is to say, on the surface the spirituals spoke of religious concerns in ways that appeared otherworldly and of no threat to the status quo. However, under this superficial message spirituals were often used to send messages of planned rebellions as well as more general critiques of the slave system. Because these two messages existed simultaneously—double-talk—only an informed body of listeners could decipher them. Below the surface these songs contained a call for divine justice, a call for equality through the transformation of a troubled situation.

The communal dimension is further exemplified through the "call and response" used in singing. This exchange between singer(s) and audience entailed the latter verbally affirming the truth and importance of the song being sung, adding lines when motivated to do so. Readers should not believe that this exchange, or the more general singing of these spirituals, was limited to formal worship experience. To the contrary, spirituals developed whenever singers believed it necessary and appropriate. This could be during a formal worship moment, a secret hush-arbor gathering, in the work fields, or during in-between time. Another communal aspect of the spirituals revolves around their place in the "ring shout." This worship moment involved a group of believers moving around in a circle, singing spirituals after the formal service concluded. One former slave described it this way:

> Some ob de sarbants, mos'ly de ole ones 'ud preach ter us. An' den de black folks 'ud git off, down in de crick bottom, er in a thic'et, an sing an' shout an' pray. Don't know why, but de w'ite folks sho' didn't like dem ring shouts de cullud folks had. De folks git shuffle, den hit gits faster, an' faster as dey gits wa'amed up; an' dey moans an' shouts; an' sinngs, an' claps, an' dance. Some ob em gits 'zauseted an' dey drop out, an' de ring gits closer. Sometimes dey sing an' shout all night.[22]

Albert Raboteau, one of the premiere interpreters of black American religion, states that a chorus of singers outside the circle would begin singing a spiritual. As one person spoke the words to the spiritual, others responded by singing the chorus and keeping time through clapping and tapping feet.[23] When performed properly, spiritual power was manifest, people got "happy in the spirit," and souls were saved.

It is true that many white revival songs are profoundly similar to spirituals, yet the differences are as strong. The most profound difference is the experience out of which the slave songs—spirituals—developed. This music is the consequence of a unique form of human oppression, the Atlantic slave trade, which is not mirrored by any of the experiences of white revivalists and their white converts. Slaves sang to counter and overcome a form of oppression white Christians had not experienced firsthand. In addition, the spirituals drew deeply from African musical sensibilities and melody formation that offered a unique expression that many white observers (and some blacks) found "odd" and unappealing. A seldom explored possibility is that white Christians learned a musical form from enslaved Africans and used it to forge revival songs. Notions of white superiority in all things cultural, however, would have made it difficult for early white commentators on this musical form to make that admission. Finally, even when spirituals resulted from the adaptation of white hymns, they exhibited a unique tone and texture. In many ways the typical rules of language and grammar were altered to fit the sensibilities, context, and aesthetics of Africans, and the lexicon whites were familiar with was creatively manipulated by those who learned English in a less than inviting place and way.

Traditional Gospel

As independent black churches developed and gained some social standing, many black ministers objected to the spirituals, labeling them "cornfield ditties." They opposed the music's style and the manner in which it provided a reminder of slave days more than the music's thematic content. The Black Churches' opposition to content was reserved for the music referred to as the blues. In some cases, with artists like Robert Johnson, it was rumored that musical prowess was based on a deal with the devil. But regardless of such stories, it is certain that churches objected to the "earthiness" of the blues. Churches were aligned with God, and therefore the blues must—as the opposite of the church's orientation—be aligned with the devil.[24] But many of those who sang the blues were also religious in a traditional, church-derived way. Twentieth-century born-again blues folks, most notably Thomas Andrew Dorsey, were responsible for the development of a blues-influenced form of religious music called gospel blues or gospel music that got under way in 1921 with Dorsey's first song, "Someday, Somewhere." In 1931 Dorsey developed the nation's first gospel choir at Ebenezer Baptist Church in Chicago. One year later he founded the National Convention of Gospel Choirs and Choruses. This organization, although affiliated with one denomination, the National Baptist Convention, U.S.A., Inc., brought gospel music to a national audience through its workshops for choir directors and its annual meetings. Furthermore, gospel music became a part of Black Church worship because Dorsey and gospel singer Sallie Martin traveled across the nation singing and helping congregations develop gospel choirs.

Although the term *gospel music* was used by white evangelists and numerous black churches before Dorsey, he is considered the father of gospel music because of the way in which his arrangements for soloists, quartets, and other small groups ushered in the golden or classical age of a musical style that blends jazz, blues, and ragtime with the Christian message. Initially troubled by the blues influence found in the music, black churches came to embrace it when Mahalia Jackson, Clara Ward, and groups such as the Five Blind Boys and the Dixie Humming Birds spread it through concert performances and Sunday services beginning in the 1930s. According to Mahalia Jackson, black churches could not maintain their objection to the music because of its popularity:

> The more gospel singing took hold in Chicago and around the country, the more some of the colored ministers objected to it. They were cold to it. They didn't like the hand-clapping and the stomping and they said we were bringing jazz into the church and it wasn't dignified. . . . In those days the big colored churches didn't want me and they didn't let me in. I had to make it my business to pack the little basement-hall congregations and storefront churches and get their respect that way. When they began to see the crowds I drew, the big churches began to sit up and take notice.[25]

As the music grew in popularity, the published musical scores, first generated by Dorsey's publishing house, made it possible for local churches to incorporate gospel songs into their order of worship. Most contemporary black churches still use classical gospel during worship because of its strong and hope-filled lyrics and its appeal to older members of congregations, whose numbers remain high in the Black Church.

Modern and Contemporary Gospel Music

Figures such as those named above dominated gospel music until the late 1960s and 1970s, when the influence of new secular music was felt. The limited use of instruments in traditional gospel was replaced by attention to synthesizers and other high-tech musical devices as well as more attention to mainstream outlets like radio and film. Figures such as Andre Crouch began producing music drawing heavily from the funk movement of George Clinton.[26] Traditional gospel had its greatest appeal among black Christians, those who already embraced the church, while contemporary gospel crossed over into an unchurched audience.

Although first developed in the Baptist church and "refined" in Pentecostal circles through the introduction of R & B influences, gospel music is appreciated and claimed across denominational lines. It became the defining expression of musical devotion to God, and in many churches gospel music replaced the spirituals. Furthermore, unlike the spirituals, gospel music appealed outside the formal church services as gospel records became staples of home devotion. Thousands of records were sold through both secular and Christian music shops across the nation. As the late twentieth century approached, the appeal of this music continued to grow, fueled in part by artists such as Shirley Caesar, who moved gospel from its classical style to a "modern" formation marked by new arrangements and the use of instruments such as drums and guitars as opposed to just piano and organ. New musical arrangements, however, were placed within the context of traditional lyrics that stated black Christian doctrine in explicit ways.

The development of modern gospel was also fueled by social conditions. As scholar of black religion Melva Costen says, "The civil rights movement deepened the awareness of societal inequalities, and attention was focused again on the 'beloved community,' which could be brought together through music. The electric organ, with its vibrato capabilities, and microphones that had invaded the worship space expanded the quality of sound, style, and mechanics of delivery." This new gospel sound changed the aesthetics of black church worship as choirs imitated the music on Sundays and the choir's attire became more dramatic to complement the more explosive sound.[27] Gospel singing preacher Shirley Caesar attracts large numbers of fans, most of whom are already members of churches. This was also the case for one of the gospel greats, Rev. James Cleveland, who founded and pastored Cornerstone Institutional Baptist Church in Los Angeles.[28]

Success resulted in the presence of market forces shaping the music that has troubled some traditional artists and church members. Complaints only increased as modern gospel gave way to a more contemporary sound, which incorporated rock, funk, pop, and country western with the lyrics of modern gospel. A central figure in this shift from modern to contemporary gospel is Andre Crouch of the Church of God in Christ. After touring with a choir he created in the late 1960s, Crouch developed a new group called the Disciples and began his unique blend of musical styles. According to many black Christians and musicians, this new form of gospel was losing its connection to the Black Church and gaining a greater dependence on secular music executives. Unlike earlier forms of gospel, it did not limit its audience to Christians. Rather, its embrace of contemporary and secular musical styles combined with the old message in a more subtle form appealed to those outside the Church as well. Concerning this, Albertina Walker, a founding member of the quartet the Caravans, says: "One while, they were calling it rock gospel, then it was inspirational gospel, and then pop gospel. Now, it's contemporary gospel. . . . The record companies want you to do the kind of music they feel they can make money off of, and if you want to make a living as a singer, you have to go along with the music part of it."[29] Some have suggested that contemporary gospel has lost sight of the music's purpose and message. Concerning this, Rev. Milton Brunson, a well-known traditional gospel artist and leader of the Thompson Community Singers of Chicago, says: "The contemporary sound is a ballroom beat, when you're sitting here listening to it you never get any spiritual feeling. When you sing the songs like Mahalia Jackson and James Cleveland used to sing . . . oh, it's a whole different thing."[30]

Despite objections from some, the mass appeal of contemporary gospel music has resulted in an expanded audience. Churches have recognized contemporary gospel and are using it as a tool for evangelizing communities. During the 1980s many churches nurtured choirs for more than the music they provided. Black Pentecostal churches are noteworthy for the growth of contemporary gospel within their ranks, in part because of fewer prohibitions against the use of musical instruments during worship. So, for example, churches such as Washington Temple COGIC (Brooklyn, New York) nurtured gospel choirs that recorded albums and filled pews. People would come from across the city to hear the choir sing, and they became a somewhat captive audience for sermons. And the Pentecostal singing group The Clark Sisters brought additional attention to the COGIC and its musical gifts. Many churches in fact experienced growth based on the popularity of their choirs. Hence, excellent choir directors were in as much demand as charismatic preachers, and most churches now make it their business to nurture at least one choir with an understanding that there is a direct relationship between good music and full pews.

In short, complaints by black churches point to contemporary gospel's attempt to reach the unchurched, to draw them in by avoiding a message of repentance and salvation that is too confrontational. Christians interested in the music have to come to terms with a more subtle message of Jesus Christ and the merits of salvation, a form of the Christian message with a new set of influences ranging from post–civil rights politics to the aesthetics of R & B and hip hop culture. The connection is actually quite clear:

Historically, most R & B singers have grown up singing in church; still today, artists from Snoop to Lil' Kim have sung in the choir as kids. And the two genres have met in the middle any number of times, from the Teddy Riley-produced Return by the Winans, in 1990, to L. L. Cool J's 1991 track "The Power of God.". . . The Edwin Hawkins Singers' "Oh, Happy Day" was a chart smash in 1972, and the Clark Sisters' "You Brought the Sunshine" lit up discos in 1982. And who could forget M. C. Hammer's 1990 "Pray"?[31]

Gospel Meets Hip Hop

The most widely discussed and debated artist of the late twentieth century is probably Kirk Franklin, founder of Kirk Franklin and the Family as well as God's Property. Franklin has developed a unique musical form that, like Andre Crouch during the 1970s and 1980s, samples current musical trends and blends them with the message of the gospel worded in slang. In addition, Franklin and his groups appear in the fashion and style of the late twentieth century. It is not uncommon for Franklin to sport vanguard designer wear and members of the group to flash fashions by urban designers such as FUBU and Phatfarm. The hip hop influence is further pronounced through rap stars in his videos and recording collaborations with rapper L. L. Cool J and hip hop artist R. Kelly.[32] The appeal of Kirk Franklin is undeniable. For example, Franklin's 1997 album "God's Property from Kirk Franklin's Nu Nation" made it to number one on the Billboard R & B chart and sold over 2 million copies (double platinum), and he is the best-selling gospel artist to ever record an album.[33] Kirk Franklin is "big time," so to speak, selling out major venues across the nation. While his style embraces hip hop culture, Franklin's message remains true to the agenda outlined in the spirituals and traditional gospel. The influence contemporary gospel music has had on church worship is now coupled with the influence of Franklin and musicians like him. Their sound and embrace of popular culture appeal to young people and have resulted in a forced rethinking of what a Christian "looks like" and what the proper ways to worship are. This move requires a rejection of reactionary and stereotyped depictions of youth culture. On this point, Franklin says: "Many times, when people see the clothes, the jewelry—they see a drug dealer. Or if I tell them I do music, it's gotta be rap when in fact I'm a 25-year-old minister who loves God. . . . I'm dedicated to God and I'm working like sweat to make sure that every word that I sing I can effectively put into practice."[34]

The Function of Music in Worship

Regardless of where one goes, the particular denomination does not matter, music is a central component of black worship. Drawing inspiration from the Old Testament book of Psalms, black churches attempt to "sing unto the LORD a new song; sing unto the LORD, all the earth! Sing unto the LORD, bless his name" (Ps 96:1-2). From more formal hymns sung by the entire congregation, to songs by the choir, to solos, black churches use music to express the content of their faith—love for God and hope for the renewal of life. In some respects music is used in worship as a way of expressing this faith and regenerating spiritual strength. Mahalia Jackson, a major figure in gospel music, speaks to this point, saying that "'testifying' to music in church and 'getting happy' with singing has always been a way in which the Negro has sought to renew his strength." While vital within the formal context of worship, religious music's function extends into the secular realm as well. Jackson speaks to this within the context of the struggle for civil rights when she says: "Many colored people in the South have been kept down so hard that they have had little schooling. They can't handle a lot of reading, but as one preacher said, 'the singing has drawn them together. Through the songs they have expressed years of suppressed hopes, suffering and even joy and love.'"[35]

Although this expression of faith is vital, music also serves a less spiritual purpose by marking the various phases of worship. For example, the start of service is announced by singing a song, such as the hymn "We've Come This Far by Faith," which alerts the congregation of the transition from mundane time for greeting friends and preparing for worship to sacred time for fellowship with God. Other important segments of the service such as prayer, the sermon, and communion are transitioned into through music as well. These songs help members of the congregation shift moods. This use of music as a marker for various portions of the worship experience is common across denominational lines. What is less consistent, however, is the role of musical instruments during worship. Whereas most churches with financial means will have a piano and organ, some will also have drums, guitars, tambourines, and more. While present in some Methodist and Baptist churches, Pentecostal churches were probably the first to see the merit in a large range of instruments. Turning again to the Psalms, many supported the decision to use instruments like drums by reference to the following words:

> Praise ye the LORD. Praise God in his sanctuary: praise
>   him in the firmament of his power.
> Praise him for his mighty acts: praise him according to
>   his excellent greatness.
> Praise him with the sound of the trumpet: praise him
>   with the psaltery and harp.

> Praise him with the timbrel and dance: praise him with
>   stringed instruments and organs.
> Praise him upon the loud cymbals: praise him upon the
>   high sounding cymbals. (Ps 150:1-5)

Many churches frowned on the use of so many instruments thinking them best suited for secular bands. Using them, the argument went, turned church worship into a disco. With time, however, churches that initially opposed instruments beyond the piano, organ, hands, and human voices softened their stance. Whether churches use two or twenty instruments during worship, almost all black churches draw from two musical traditions: the spirituals and gospel.

Preaching in the Black Sermonic Tradition

It is likely that the black sermonic style (black preaching) first emerged during the mid-1700s, when slaves combined elements of African orality with the aesthetics and content of camp meeting preaching by George Whitfield and others.[36] Formal training, restricted and unnecessary at this point, was of little consideration. A literate member of the congregation would read the scripture, and the preacher would give the sermon. In other cases the sermon was given based upon the preacher's ability to remember scripture and stories once heard, or from a limited reading ability secured in opposition to formal regulations. As one former slave recounted:

> De preacher I laked de bes' was name Mathew Swing. . . . An' he sho' could read out of his han'. He neber larned no real readin' an' writin' but he sho' knowed his Bible and would hol' his han' out an' mak lak he was readin' an' preach de purtiest preachin' you ever heered.[37]

Preaching success was openly expressed through the congregation "talking back" ("call and response") during the sermon. "Amen!" or "Preach!" remains a part of this "call and response" tradition that affirms the truth of the minister's words, as something about the information provided and the style of delivery capture the imagination of listeners. As one observer noted, the best preachers "acquire a remarkable memory of words, phrases, and forms; a curious sort of poetic talent is developed, and a habit is obtained of rhapsodizing and exciting furious emotions." Another person's comment about a preacher in North Carolina also would apply to numerous others: "In his sermons there is often a clearness of statement, an earnestness of address, a sublimity and splendor of imagery, together with a deep pathos, which give his public addresses great power."[38]

Sermon Content and Purpose

Within visible and formal black churches the preacher and the preached word took the central position in worship, providing important information on and critiques of major spiritual and material concerns. In this way the preacher and sermon served as the religious, political, social, and cultural linchpin for the local church community. Preaching provided one of the few opportunities to raise questions and was one of the few avenues for authority within the antebellum period. In what position could an African exercise authority over whites but as a preacher within the church? Whereas some black preachers gave sermons that supported the "slaves be obedient" status quo, others laced their religious rhetoric with judgments of the slave system. Still others, when possible, wedded their knowledge of the Bible to the daily struggles of the slave community.[39]

Recognized as important, what do these sermons do and what are the mechanics guiding their delivery? From the beginnings of the sermonic tradition to the present, the basic purpose of the sermon has been twofold: (1) to glorify God and bring people into the church; and (2) to provide information, drawn from scripture, relevant for daily living. To accomplish this twofold agenda, ministers make strong use of several key elements, whether the sermon is developed in light of a particular theme, a particular passage (short or long) of scripture, or the telling of a biblically derived story in narrative form. Furthermore, these elements are used regardless of whether the preacher is male or female, and their use tends to cut across geographic and denominational lines. They are: (1) scripture and interpretation; (2) black history; (3) current events; (4) communal experience or history of the particular denomination and local church; (5) personal experience; (6) popular culture; and (7) the world of nature.

Scripture is the key to this process in that scriptural stories and lessons provide the basic moral and ethical norms upon which the black Christian community seeks to operate. Within the doctrine of various black denominations, scripture is upheld as the basic guide for life and, from the period of slavery on, black Christians have recognized the need for interpretations of scripture sensitive to their circumstances. Hence, it only makes sense that preachers draw heavily from these stories and present them in ways that reflect the concerns of the congregation and larger black community. In so doing preachers draw on the rich history of biblical interpretation by which Africans first explored and critiqued their enslavement. The exploration of concerns through the lens of scripture remains a trait of black preaching, as ministers juxtapose biblical personalities and contemporary black experience. Bishop John Bryant of the AME Church, for instance, had this to say concerning the suffering of humanity outlined in Romans 8:16-18:

> Abraham had to go through the trauma of almost sacrificing his own son so the world might know that God must come first. Job had to suffer physical affliction so that the world might know, "He may not come when you want him, but he's always on time." The Hebrews had to struggle for forty years in the wilderness so we might learn that only the faithful are delivered. Martin Luther King, Jr., had to experience an early death so men everywhere might know that evil men may destroy the dreamer, but they cannot destroy the dream.[40]

Concern for the larger black community, within sermons like Bryant's, must be eventually directed to the needs and issues of a particular congregation. To do so, the minister might discuss, for example, Christ's calling of the disciples to the mission and the work agenda of the local church. Or, the Hebrew Bible discussion on tithing might be related to the need for those on the local level to contribute 10 percent of their income to the church. Regardless of the scenario, according to Baptist minister Gardner Taylor, "there is a theme which runs through the Bible and through life. The preacher or the believer who misses this never gets hold of Biblical truth in its full sweep and scope. Such a one may be said to have thoughts about the Bible, but lacks a grasp of its thought and thrust."[41]

Related to the above concern with context, sermons over the past three decades reflect the changing definitions and sensibilities of the black community. In other words, black sermons in recent years have shown an increased sensitivity to women demonstrated, in many cases, through an increased use of inclusive language. This is particularly so with seminary-trained ministers encountering women and men in the Academy who challenge the sexism inherent in exclusive language and who, in their writing and work with students, seek to move beyond gender-bound theological language. Many ministers are recognizing what Baptist minister Samuel D. Proctor expressed in 1996:

> Jesus defied the norm that stood in awe of the rich, the mighty, and the powerful, blessing the poor, the meek, and the pure in heart.

Thus the Christian pastor approaches the issue of diversity looking for those in the mix who have become marginalized, who had a slower beginning, and who need to catch up. The pastor knows about colonialism, slavery, sexism, racism, and classism, and about generational and pandemic poverty. In the midst of the diversity, the mind of Christ tells him or her to look for the least, the lost, and the left behind.[42]

Although this sensitivity is growing with respect to male preachers, theologian Cheryl Sanders concludes, based on a study of published sermons, that women are much more likely to use inclusive language, avoiding terms such as "he" and "Father" in reference to God and rejecting the term "man" as a reference to all people.[43] The use of inclusive language challenges contemporary black denominations in the same manner that the racial depiction of Jesus Christ (for example, a white *vs.* black painting of Jesus) was a hot topic in the 1960s. In both cases theological language and imagery are reevaluated because of what they say (or do not say) about the personhood and subjectivity of all black Americans.

To further develop sermonic context, ministers give personal examples, events from their life, as illustration of the sermon's theme. Rev. Johnny Ray Youngblood, pastor of New York's Saint Paul Community Baptist Church, provides an example of this approach. In a sermon dealing with Mary, the mother of Jesus—a teenage mother—and the beauty that can come from unlikely situations, Youngblood provides an autobiographical note:

> Don't look at me funny. Please don't look at me funny. Cause, y'all, I went to college, and I didn't spend all my times in the boys' dormitory. Oh, it's good to get this stuff off your chest. And, yes, I've had some frightening moments. And even now, when I prepare this message, I can't prepare a message where I'm clear, where I'm in the clear and I'm straight and I tell y'all what y'all oughta do. This thing is a two-edged sword. It whips back and cuts the hell out of me and then comes forward and cuts y'all. And the truth of God's word is not predicated on my lifestyle. It is predicated on God's word itself.[44]

It is not uncommon to have members of the church state in casual conversation the importance of having this personal experience shared as a way of humanizing preachers who are often thought of as "larger than life." Sharing personal experience in this way allows ministers to create a sense of commonality, of solidarity, and allows congregants to think of their struggles as communal challenges. It provides a form of vulnerability that many preachers argue creates a stronger connection between the preached word and the congregation.

Furthermore, to attract young people to church, many ministers make use of slang in the preaching context and will also make use of illustrations from popular culture. For some, this entails references to hip hop culture, or recent movie releases, or new books on the market. The goal is to demonstrate the religious sensibilities present in popular culture and to demonstrate the manner in which "being in the world but not of the world" does not mean a complete rejection of secular life. At its core this appeal to popular culture for examples and illustrations of biblical precedent is in keeping with an old principle of black preaching: the language and imagery of sermons should be understandable, because they relate to the lived experience and language of the people. Rev. Youngblood is noted for this ability, but there are others who also engage in this practice. Although he is not a member of a historically black denomination, Dr. Jeremiah A. Wright, Jr., pastor of Trinity United Church of Christ in Chicago, is an exemplar of this approach and serves as a good example of the general practice as it is used in both black denominations as well as black churches in white denominations. In a 1986 sermon titled "If Only He Knew . . . " interpreting Luke 7:36-50, Wright addresses the life of an underprivileged and uninvited woman seeking transformation during a dinner party thrown by Simon the Pharisee. He says:

> No one knows how she got to be the way she was;
> She just was what she was.
> Her heart might have been broken by a no good dude
>   somewhere back in her past.
> Her life might have been messed up by some old, slick
>   sucker who turned her out at a tender age.
> Her self-esteem might have been damaged by some old
>   dummy who told her you ain't no good, you ain't
>   nothin' and you never will be. You just like your
>   daddy; he was trifflin' and you trifflin'.
> Her image of her personhood might have been marred
>   by the dominant culture's consistently telling her
>   that she and her worth were measured by how
>   she looked and not how she lived. . . .
> How do people get to be how they are?
> How did you get to be how you are?[45]

Finally, ministers often make use of moral and ethical lessons drawn from the natural environment. In this way human life is related to the rest of creation. An example of this is the famous "The Eagle Stirreth Her Nest" sermon by the late Rev. Clarence L. Franklin of New Bethel Baptist Church in Detroit. In preaching this sermon Franklin related the manner in which the eagle trains her young to fly and live within their natural environment to the manner in which God trains Christians:

> And when the eaglets are born she goes out and brings in food to feed them. And when they get to the point where they are old enough to be out on their own, why, the eagle will begin to pull out some of that down and let some of those thorns come through so that the nest won't be so comfortable. And when they get to lounging around and rolling around, the thorns prick them here and there. . . . And you know that God has to do that to us sometimes. Things are going so well, we are so satisfied we just lounge around and forget to pray.[46]

Finally, the belief that God is involved in the sermon, providing inspiration and guidance, does not take away from the fact that ministers must make themselves ready to preach. For many, this involves reading, prayer, meditation, and study. Yet what is interesting about this preparation is the manner in which it seems to enhance rather than detract from a sense of ease of delivery and freedom of expression. That is to say, the freedom of expression and movement demonstrated by the preacher within this black sermonic style reflects a general appreciation of fluidity with respect to religious ritual held by local churches. The following statement is a common expression of the attitude toward worship in more general terms: The Spirit of God, not the clock, sets the agenda.

Sermonic Style: The "Whoop"

It has been the concern of many black preachers to excite the congregation and have it respond to the spoken word with energy and gusto. The response of the congregation is referred to as "shouting" and the preacher's performance is called "whooping," or sing-song, or chanting. This is a rhythmically stylized presentation of the gospel message in which the preacher, with creative illustrations, bodily movement, changes in voice (intonations), and dramatic appeal (often including signature statements), makes the point. With the preached sermon, the minister begins in a mild tone and gradually increases the strength and excitement of the voice until reaching a climax marked by exaggerated gestures and booming voice. As scholar of black preaching Henry Mitchell puts it: "The strength of the Black tradition at its best has the ability to combine fresh insight with impact—to feed the people and yet to shake them into a recognition that the spirit of God is always moving, always dynamic. It is never weak or apologetic."[47] It is this component—the whoop—of many sermons that is probably the most hotly debated aspect of the black sermonic tradition. Both pro and con arguments claim tradition, history and even scripture to support their point, and the argument has raged for better than a century. Some claim that the whoop is performance that takes away from what should be a thoughtful presentation of scripture for a contemporary context.

Those who champion the whoop argue that it is a vital component of tradition that enhances the interaction between the preacher and the congregation. With respect to this, Henry Mitchell's writing is insightful: "The Black preacher must be not only a teacher and mobilizer, a father figure and an enabler, but also a celebrant. He must have a little of the joy. . . . It must be clear that he is filled by the same joy he declares to his congregation."[48] The congregation speaks its approval of the message through shouts of "Amen!" "Preach it!" "Say that!" and other exclamations. At times, and in some cases, ministers will call for a response from the congregation with expressions such as "Can I get a witness!" or "I wish you would pray with me." The request for participation can also be much more straightforward: "Somebody say amen!" The minister will hesitate, awaiting the requested response. At times, a pause is enough, without the verbal request, to elicit a response from the congregation. A typical "call and response" might go something like this:

> Preacher: God is good!
> Congregants: Amen! Preach!
> Preacher: God will make a way out of no way!
> Congregants: Well . . . !
> Preacher: Can I get a witness? Say amen somebody!
> Congregants: Amen, preacher!

Testimony in the Black Church

Preaching requires a calling, a heartfelt assertion that God has selected the person for ministry. However, the black denominations discussed in this volume also hold a belief in the priesthood of all believers that gives opportunity—and in many ways requires—all believers to discuss their relationship to God in front of others. This public declaration—the layperson's sermon—is called a testimony. Retelling one's "story"can take place as part of the formal structure of a worship service or during special services such as prayer meetings. Testimonies are said to address three major topics, all or any combination of which may be present: (1) discussion of the believer's conversion and/or sanctification; (2) proclamation of his or her triumph over difficulties; and (3) a request for prayer because the believer struggles with a particular difficulty. When addressing any or all of these elements, God is always given thanks for blessings received (as simple as continued life) and blessings expected.

With respect to discussion of one's conversion, there is a long tradition, beginning around the time of the first Great Awakening, of converts sharing their stories as a means of expressing their gratitude to God and as a way of encouraging others to live their faith. It was not uncommon for enslaved converts to develop special times for the sharing of such experiences. In this way they were able to prove the transformation that had taken place by attesting to it in public, before the assembly of converts who could measure the account against their own. The sharing of these testimonies provided a liminal period of sorts, a time between times, during which the power of God was linguistically affirmed and often physically felt anew. An example of the tone of such a conversion as provided by an ex-slave goes this way:

> When God struck me dead with his power I was living on Fourteenth Avenue. It was the year of the Centennial. I was in my house alone, and I declare unto you, when his power struck me I died. I fell out on the floor flat on my back. I could neither speak nor move, for my tongue stuck to the roof of my mouth; my jaws were locked and my limbs were stiff. In my vision I saw hell and the devil. I was crawling along a high brick wall, it seems, and it looked like I would fall into a dark, roaring pit. I looked away to the east and saw Jesus.[49]

Note the vivid language used to describe this experience. Through graphic depictions of the horrors of being unsaved and the struggle to obtain salvation, converts in their testimonies are able to demonstrate the weight of mundane existence and the glory of renewed life in Christ. It is usually recounted as a powerful experience. For example, Richard Allen, mentioned in the discussion of the AME Church, spoke of his experience as a time during which "his dungeon shook and his chains fell off." Countless others would agree with the urgency of his language. The challenge, however, is to capture in words a profoundly mystical and metaphysical occurrence that usually comes after some type of spiritual wrestling or trauma triggering a sense of inner need. Whether mild or powerful, there is a general horror when confronted with one's short-comings that is only subdued by a surrender to God. In other words, the person testifying had to "come bringing the news of . . . resurrection from death and hell, and . . . had to bring it straight."[50]

In years past as well as the present, rehearsing the conversion experience is typically placed in the context of thanking God for various blessings received, such as recovery from illness or receiving some unexpected money to help pay bills. All of this, whether small or large, points to God's involvement in human history. Before testimonies conclude, this rejoicing in God's activities is usually followed by a request for the support of the congregation as the testifier continues to struggle with various issues and problems. But even this mild lament is done with an overall tone of optimism. Hence, there is a cathartic or therapeutic quality to testifying that enables the person sharing and those hearing to reaffirm commitment to their faith and to the Black Church.

Giving a Testimony
There is no age limit attached to the giving of testimonies. During any given service one might see both children and adults sharing their stories of conversion. Within many local churches across the seven denominations, children are in fact trained to consider it an honor and duty to share their experience. In this way churches make an effort to grow adults who can easily witness their faith to friends and strangers, often saying something resembling this:

> Giving glory and honor to God, I thank God for allowing me to live another day. I thank God for saving my soul from sin and placing my feet on the path of righteousness. I ask that the saints pray much for me as I continue to struggle to make heaven my home.

In less formal contexts, the framework for testimonies is changed to fit the situation. For example, rather than selecting people in advance to testify, a general invitation may be issued by a worship leader.

There is no standard form for a testimony. While it is common for the person to stand and face the congregation, much about the way the testimony is given depends on how the person is "moved by the spirit." Of more importance than form or style of presentation is a basic sincerity, an indication to listeners that the experience is *true*. Members of the local church hearing the testimony understand the content and intent on a variety of levels, including some that are more intuitive than inductive. In attending services one might also encounter other forms of testimony.

Singers, for example, may use a song to express their experience with God. Or a musician might use the playing of an instrument as his or her testimony. It has also happened more than once that a congregant with liturgical dance talents has used this skill to express acceptance of and devotion to Jesus Christ. Regardless of the medium used, the basic point remains the same: the testimony is a sharing of one's transforming experience and one's daily temptations and victories over sin.

Prayer in Black Worship

In addition to songs, sermons, and testimonies, participation in worship includes prayer. From the period of slavery to the present, prayer has remained an important component of both formal and informal worship and devotion. Prayer provided, in the words of James Melvin Washington, a historian of African American religion, a "spiritual intimacy," a time of profound connection to the divine.[51] This notion is implicit in ex-slave Henry Baker's 1938 interview. According to Baker:

> Prayer is er sincere desire uv de heart. Jesus says, 'Ast whut yuh will en muh father will gib hit untuh yuh. I prays tuh de Father fer yuh.' Now ef yuh gotta sincere desire tuh wanner home, ast God en nobody aint got tuh give 'cep God. Evah thing on earth is his enn he is de Fatha uv de worl' en ast yuh Fatha whut you will en he will gib hit untuh yuh. Prayah is sumpin dat unlocks de door.[52]

As unencumbered conversation that could take place audibly or in the mind, prayer served as a means of voicing one's concerns directly to a powerful source of assistance. With the development of Pentecostalism and its focus on speaking in tongues, it was understood that prayer could take place in the dominant social language, English, or in a special tongue, a prayer language. The importance of the latter is that it represents, from the perspective of many Pentecostals, a more pure communication, one that is not tainted by the limitations of human imagination and linguistic skills. This prayer language represents the human spirit praying directly to God. Whether in tongues or not, prayer allows the person praying and those participating in the praying moment to reflect, center themselves, and focus on the divine presence, even in unlikely places. And black Christians across denominational lines acknowledge that direct communication with God is made possible through the Christ event—the death and resurrection of Jesus Christ.

Like testimonies, prayer traditionally revolves around one of several areas: (1) thanksgiving for blessings received; (2) a general recognition of and gratefulness for God's goodness; or (3) a request for a specific blessing or for general well-being. Prayer, of course, can encompass any combination of these areas. Beyond widely recognized areas of concern in prayers, there is some agreement on the possible responses to prayer. It is typically taught that God can answer prayer in three ways: (1) by granting the request; (2) by answering no and denying the request; or, (3) by responding "not yet," meaning the time is not proper for the granting of the request. Related to the three responses listed here, Christians within black churches often argue that prayers seemingly unanswered are improperly directed; that is, they are asking for something that is outside the scope of proper Christian conduct, such as a vindictive or retaliatory request. Or the prayer was said without proper faith. In any case, God is not brought into question in any sustained way.

Intent and Location of Prayer

Some might think of prayer and meditation as synonymous activities. In the Black Church they are different. Prayer within this tradition is more than quiet contemplation with its variety of possible foci—the universe, the inner self, nature, and so on. For black church communities, prayer is more directed than this because it is thanksgiving or a petition directed toward God, and God alone. Meditation involves much broader parameters of conduct and intent, related to a much more expansive understanding of spirituality. James Washington's description of what prayer requires is useful here:

> Prayer is an attempt to count the stars of our souls. Under its sacred canopy, an oratory of hope echoes the vast but immediate distance between who we are and who we want to be. This peculiar trek sentences its devotees to an arduous discipline. Prayer demands focus and obedience, as well as intimacy and faithful nurture. A certain civility is inherent in this transaction. Its requirements are both communal and individual.[53]

In general terms prayer is either private or public and performed by all converts. There is no restriction on time or length, and there are no hard and fast rules concerning how one positions the body. New converts across denominational lines are often taught that private prayer should take place continuously throughout the day and can happen while standing, seated, during leisure, or in the middle of work. In this way prayer is more than what one does; to some degree prayer becomes what one is. Put another way, the reflective relationship with God connoted by prayer is the cornerstone of one's being. It is an affirmation of one's deep, spiritual connections to the divine.

More formal prayers during the course of scheduled worship services and prayer meetings are usually a bit more structured and stylistically defined by church-derived expectations, although all praying positions—in private or public—should reflect a sense of human submission before the Christian God. For example, during Sunday services there is usually a morning prayer: one of the church members selected by the worship leader, kneels in the front of the church and prays on behalf of the entire congregation. The prayer leader is usually selected because of a special talent for effective praying, the ability "to reach the throne of God" and to make the congregation experience, feel, this connection. Particular bits of imagery are learned during the course of one's years in the Black Church, and these images and phrases—religious clichés of sorts—are commonly found in public prayers. Whether the date is 1928 or 1998, and regardless of denomination, one might hear words similar to these:

> Almighty and all-wise God . . . 'tis once more and again that a few of your beloved children are gathered together to call upon your holy name. We bow at your footstool, Master, to thank you for our spared lives. We thank you that we were able to get up this morning clothed in our right mind. For, Master, since we met here, many have been snatched out of the land of the living and hurled into eternity. But through your goodness and mercy we have been spared to assemble ourselves here once more to call upon a Captain who has never lost a battle. . . . Build us up where we are torn down, and strengthen us where we are weak.[54]

Besides this type of prayer, most services also contain an altar call—in some cases connected to the call by the preacher for people to accept Jesus as personal savior or rededicate themselves to God—during which individuals make their way to the altar in the front of the church and pray as individuals. The altar call concludes with a collective prayer led by the pastor or one of the church leaders. Outside Sunday services and hours during which the church is open for members of the community to come in and pray, many local churches hold prayer services during which testimonies are given and both collective and individual prayers are made.

Like the "call and response" of a sermon, public prayers receive a response. For example, the above prayer might have been peppered with "Amens!" in support of the prayer's petition to God and in appreciation for the sense of fiery optimism presented. Furthermore, like the sermon or the music, a particularly impassioned prayer can cause, in some churches, "shouting," through which the presence of the Holy Spirit is manifested and evidenced through energetic and rhythmic movements of the body that might include jumping in place, running, uncontrolled weeping, speaking in tongues, or fainting. The prayer might also produce a spiritual excitement that results in members of the congregation "dancing in the spirit." Like shouting, this involves the Holy Spirit taking control of the individual and manifesting this change through rhythmic movement resembling dance.

One should not believe that prayers, individual or collective, are always spiritual, without any concern for political realities. As countless slave narratives and testimonies state, slaves prayed for freedom, and the denial of opportunity to pray resulted in the development of the AME Church and its progressive agenda. This understanding of the connection between prayer and social transformation continues in black Christianity, with prime examples being the use of prayer during various sit-ins and other civil rights activities in the 1960s. One gets a more contemporary hint of this relationship in a prayer offered by AME minister Frank Madison Reid, III, given in 1994:

> O God, liberate us from the domination of individual and institutional violence. Liberate us for the ministry of deliverance to the captives within and without. Liberate us from a self-centered spiritual materialism and liberate us to serve the present age.[55]

Whether of new construction, an existing structure purchased from another congregation, or a transformed storefront, the Black Church centers around worship guided by a set of basic beliefs. Through celebration of the Church's beliefs, or worship, the Black Church announces its devotion to God and expresses the importance of religious community. Although conducted within the physical space of the church, worship and the beliefs that motivate and direct it have consequences for daily life. Celebration of one's connection with God, according to black Christians, should motivate positive interaction with others and should serve as the basis for involvement in social activism. That is to say, at its best, the Black Church's appeal to activism in its various modes of worship has translated into actual work on social issues. In the following chapters attention is turned to key areas of this activism.

PART II

THEMES IN CONTEMPORARY PRAXIS

AME Zion Church
Brooklyn, New York

4

The Black Church on Economic Issues

It was assumed that the legislation-fueled opportunities gained during the civil rights movement would secure the economic welfare of black Americans. For example, the Civil Rights Act of 1964 made discrimination in employment, federal funding of programs, and public accommodations illegal. It gave administrative weight to this through the creation of the Equal Employment Opportunity Commission (EEOC). The 1965 Voting Rights Act made discrimination with respect to the vote punishable by law. These were followed, in 1968, by another Civil Rights Act that outlawed discrimination in housing. In the 1980s and 1990s attention to civil rights was renewed through the extension of previous legislation such as the Voting Rights Act (1982), and the recodifying during 1991 of employment decisions made in 1964. Furthermore, there are more elected black officials today than during the 1960s, with many serving, during the 1980s and 1990s, as mayors of major cities (for example, David Dinkins in New York, Harold Washington in Chicago, and Tom Bradley in Los Angeles). Although promising on some level, many of these black politicians inherit tremendous fiscal and social problems within troubled cities.[1] Their mixed success within these cities serves as an apt metaphor for the post–civil rights economic standings of most black Americans.

By some accounts, in 1976, roughly 3 out of 10 black Americans were living below the poverty line as opposed to 1 out of 10 white Americans.[2] Even fixing attention on the black middle class does not brighten substantially the picture for black America. According to sociologist Orlando Patterson, "The impressive growth of the Afro-American middle class should not be used to mask the fact that, in comparative ethnic terms, the economic record is decidedly mixed. In 1995, the median income of all Afro-American families was \$25,970, which was 60.8 percent of the Euro-American median family income of \$42,646. This was only a 1.6 percent improvement on the ratio of 59.2 percent in 1967."[3]

Community Economic Development

Forging a Collective Response

The Black Church has maintained a publicly expressed commitment to changing the economic situation of black Americans. In fact, economics and politics have been the primary modes of church activism. Beginning with the work of the NCBC, official statements developed through denominational cooperation point to this commitment. For example, the "Statement of Legislative Principles" developed by the Pennsylvania Council of Churches during 1999-2000 had the support of twenty-two churches, including all seven major black denominations. And its commitment to issues of economic development is explicit:

> In a just society, each person has adequate opportunity to work for his or her own benefit and for the community. The whole of society is strengthened as its members know themselves to be full participants in and contributors to the common good. The failure of a society to provide adequate opportunities for gainful employment condemns a portion of its people to poverty and weakens the very fabric of community life. We support the empowerment of all people to obtain employment that provides economic self-sufficiency and to enjoy economic opportunity. God ordains work as a part of human life, and it is to be honored and rewarded. Through work, human dignity is enhanced and material benefits are acquired. The encouragement of employment opportunities with livable wages and benefits is one of the most important activities of government.[4]

Concerning welfare, the council implicitly rejects analyses that blame victims for their economic hardships. Rather, the council calls for reform that provides "adequate income supports and other human services" while those capable of work seek meaningful and sound employment. Once employment is sought, twenty-four-hour-a-day child care should be in place to safeguard children while their parents earn a living. In addition, while recognizing the somewhat unpredictable nature of our economy based on shifting work forces, resources, and other factors, the council calls for government regulations that would allow for a more effective conversion of facilities to new forms of work in light of current shifts from industry to service and high technology work. This will enable an efficient conversion of local and regional economies based on market forces and other factors. As a final element of this project, the council proposes the taxation process be revamped so that "income tax exclude income sufficient to place reporting households above poverty guidelines."[5]

In addition to cross denominational attention to economic hardship in black communities, particular denominations have also made statements that set their agenda and vision for improvement. The Progressive National Baptist Convention, for example, understands its development as a movement toward social activism. According to its statement "Civil Rights Advocacy and Activism," this thrust continues as "new generations of Progressive Baptists are continuing the struggle for full voter registration, education and participation, affirmative action against all forms of racism and bigotry, Black economic empowerment and development, equal educational opportunity."[6]

The National Baptist Convention, U.S.A., Inc., and the National Baptist Convention of America made a similar commitment to the economic welfare of black Americans through the formation of the Minority Enterprise Financial Acquisition Corp., which provides financial assistance with the building of low-cost housing. According to one of the ministers involved in this corporation: "We want to change the whole face of blighted areas of urban America. No longer can we afford the luxury of standing in our pulpits moaning and groaning the Gospel. We've got to build housing, day care centers and shopping centers so we can employ our own."[7]

The Church of God in Christ maintains a similar commitment as a point of mandatory ministry. Its "Goals for the Year 2000 and Beyond" as expressed by the missions division includes this statement: "To provide better financial assistance in areas where there is severe economic hardship." The social transformation thrust is continued with respect to the activities local churches are encouraged to undertake:

To promote home missions by encouraging the local church to do the following:
A. Engage in activities to build/restore the family unit
B. Engage in mission and development of the community
C. Engage in active street, prison, jail, and nursing-home ministries.[8]

From the above it is clear that at least rhetorically the Black Church is committed to improving the economic condition of black Americans. Among the most visible strategies by which it sought during the late twentieth century to influence the economic resources of black Americans involved: (1) electing officials sympathetic to its agenda; and (2) promoting cross- denominational organizations such as Operation PUSH (People United to Save Humanity).

The movement of black clergy into political office is an old strategy used to advance black Americans by changing the complexion, so to speak, of the political order. Initially, Reconstruction made this possible, and clergy such as Henry McNeal Turner of the AME Church gained political positions within various southern states. However, continuing racial discrimination prevented these church leaders from exercising the authority their offices should have entailed. After the civil rights movement, there was another and more beneficial push toward elected office. A prime example of this level of public involvement, Rev. Adam Clayton Powell, Jr., was already mentioned. But there are numerous others—mayors such as Rev. Noel C. Taylor of Roanoke, Virginia; Rev. Walter E. Fountroy, former congressman from Washington, D.C.; Rev. Floyd Flake, former congressman from Queens; and Rev. Benjamin Hooks, who served as a judge in Tennessee before leading the NAACP (starting in 1977). The Church of God in Christ, often considered more politically conservative than the other denominations, has also had its share of political leaders. Among them are Robert L. Harris, the first black state legislator in Utah; J. O. Patterson, Jr., the first black state senator in Tennessee since Reconstruction; and Samuel Jackson, who served as assistant secretary of Housing and Urban Development during the 1970s.[9] These political leaders and others like them used their religious sensibilities as a way of shaping governmental policies for the welfare of the underprivileged. In addition to these office holders, it is also important to mention Rev. Jesse Jackson's 1984 and 1988 presidential campaigns. It is estimated that Jackson's candidacy resulted in millions registering to vote, and in the 1988 national election he received roughly seven million votes. Supported by numerous religious leaders, including the president of the National Baptist Convention, U.S.A., Inc., and the presiding bishop of the Church of God in Christ, his campaign served to push issues facing black Americans to a prominent place in the Democratic convention's national platform.

Outside of individual office holders and beyond the inroads made by a declining Southern Christian Leadership Conference (SCLC) now headed by Martin Luther King, III, Operation PUSH is probably one of the more visible church-based organizations for social transformation.

Formed in 1971 by Jesse Jackson, the organization has committed itself to the economic progress of the underprivileged through four major projects: voter registration, economic development, education, and international developments (civil rights *and* human rights).[10] In 1996, Operation PUSH merged with the more diverse National Rainbow Coalition to form the Rainbow PUSH Action Network, an organization that combines the former's economic thrust with the more general concern with equality shown by the latter. During the meeting announcing this merger, Jackson gave a concise statement of the new organization's mission: "The Rainbow PUSH Action Network is going to boycott, negotiate, vote and march our way to a better Chicago [its headquarters is located there], a better Illinois, a better America."[11] Although the agenda remains the same—economic and social progress for the oppressed—the constituency was extended by the merger to more widely represent various communities of color. There are plans to even extend the organization to address economic issues related to the Pacific Rim.

Local Church Solutions

Although the perspectives assumed by denominations with respect to economic issues are important, it is really on the local level that one best measures the activism of the Black Church. As recent studies by Andrew Billingsley and by C. Eric Lincoln and Lawrence Mamiya attest, local black churches are involved in changing the condition of black Americans. According to Billingsley's study, roughly two-thirds of the churches surveyed sponsor outreach programs. Methodist churches tend to be the most active, followed by Baptist conventions (particularly the Progressive National Baptist Convention) and Pentecostal churches such as the Church of God in Christ.[12] With respect to local activities, there are several approaches to economic development and the elimination of poverty that surface consistently: (1) business ventures and job development; (2) housing; and (3) education.

Looking at the needs of their particular communities, some churches, for example, have opened restaurants, food stores, high-tech industry, garment production, and gas stations. Allen AME Church in New York is a prime example of this activity. Rev. Floyd Flake decided that the church, with its financial resources, must play a major role in the economic revitalization of its community. To do this, Allen purchased a block-long commercial district in Queens and transformed the dilapidated area into a collection of thriving businesses including legal offices, a restaurant, and a drug store with a total value of 50 million dollars.[13] Another innovative approach is that taken by Mount Olivet Baptist

Church of St. Paul, Minnesota. The church spearheaded an effort to buy almost one hundred miles of railroad track and form the Minnesota Valley Transportation Co., Inc., Southwest. It is the largest minority-owned railroad company in the United States.[14] Rather than owning businesses, other churches encourage members to think about entrepreneurial opportunities. For example, business prospects were recently listed in the Sunday bulletin for Bridge Street AME Church:

> Shouldn't you own a business? The Neighborhood Franchise Project is putting people in business in Bedford-Stuyvesant. You can get a low interest loan for up to 90% of the cost of starting proven franchise businesses. Individuals eligible to apply include members of Bridge Street Church, their family and friends, residents of Central Brooklyn and anyone committed to starting business and creating jobs in Bedford-Stuyvesant. . . . For more information, call Bridge Street Development Corporation.[15]

Churches in various denominations also provide start-up funds for small businesses based on church resources such as credit unions as well as through loans arranged by their business development staff. In addition, many churches cooperate with the Department of Housing and Urban Development to accomplish their economic goals. Still others engage in economic development and community revitalization through a combination of the above financial sources. Once those interested in entrepreneurial opportunities are identified and financial resources provided, churches such as First AME Church of Los Angeles offer technological assistance. The Entrepreneurial Training Program (part of the Business Resource Center) of First AME Church has helped more than eight hundred start-up businesses. In addition to this type of assistance, the Business Resource Center also contains a library with information on grant opportunities as well as materials that help with the writing of business plans.

In order to help members of the congregation monitor and manage their money, many churches are creating credit unions. Although useful at that level, churches are finding that credit unions typically do not provide the capital necessary for large-scale development projects. Therefore, what credit unions mean for the economic health and growth of black Americans remains an open question. For example, according to some ministers credit-union loans are used for personal convenience (consumer consumption) as opposed to economic growth. To counter this, Concord Baptist Church, for example, decided that its Federal Credit Union would change its lending practices and give greater attention to applicants interested in venture capital and business-based community development.[16]

Many churches are working with consulting firms to provide financial planning and other needed finance-related services for blacks who have achieved some level of security. A recent issue of *Emerge Magazine* provided an interesting example of this process. Montel Hill, president and CEO of H & R Consulting is working with church leaders in the Baltimore area to introduce congregations to insurance and retirement plans. Efforts such as those initiated by H & R Consulting also entail helping churches develop the financial base necessary to undertake outreach activities with little external assistance. Beyond these services, Charles L. Kennedy's African American Business Foundation, headquartered in Tampa, attempts to keep dollars within black communities by distributing goods and services to churches by catalog. According to Kennedy, this serves as an opportunity to generate start-up funds for business ventures within the communities serviced by black churches.[17] It is not surprising that some churches are moving in the direction of financial management and credit. In some local cases they are merely following the lead of the parent body. For example, the AME Church recently made available to members an unsecured Visa Card. The CME Church is also sponsoring a credit card; for every three thousand dollars spent on the card the denomination receives twenty dollars.[18]

Shifts in the economy away from industrial jobs to those in the service and high-technology sectors left many blacks unable to compete for jobs requiring specialized training. Black churches within urban areas are particularly exposed to this dilemma. Realizing that jobs provide financial possibilities that enliven communities, black churches are attempting to "grow" jobs. In part this is accomplished through business ventures. But beyond this, many of the larger black churches also develop job banks that allow them to tap into city and state opportunities for employment. First AME Church of Los Angeles has one of the best such programs. Using a primarily volunteer staff, it contacts potential employers and makes them aware of the church's applicant database. Through this process of locating and screening potential employees, the church had placed roughly eighteen hundred people in jobs by 1994. In addition, the church sponsors job fairs.[19]

From the Great Migration to the present the urbanization of black Americans has had benefits, but it has also resulted in economic hardships expressed in part through substandard housing. Local churches, recognizing this dilemma, initiated subsidized housing. An example is the Nehemiah Homes Project (of the East Brookly Congregations—EBC), developed by fifty congregations in East Brooklyn during the early 1980s and chaired by Rev. Johnny Ray Youngblood of Saint Paul Community Baptist Church. Like the biblical figure Nehemiah, who rebuilt Jerusalem after its destruction, this project is concerned with rebuilding black neighborhoods. It is affiliated with the national organization known as the Industrial Areas Foundation (IAF), which has two aims: (1) to generate the construction of affordable housing; and (2) to develop a national minimum salary of twenty-five thousand dollars.[20] Initially started with modest aims, the group pushed New York City to cleanup neighborhoods, renovate parks, and replace missing street signs. Now the Nehemiah Project is responsible for more than two thousand houses in Brooklyn, made possible through donations from participating churches as well as their denominations. The Nehemiah Project argues that proper and affordable housing ties people to neighborhoods and generates a sense of ownership and pride. This, in turn, counters feelings of hopelessness and despair generated by war-zone-like urban crises. In the words of one Nehemiah homeowner, Vida Griffith: "Before, you wouldn't want to walk down the street here [Alabama Avenue in East Brooklyn], you'd be so afraid. . . . This is a dream come true for minority people like us, who can't afford those mansions out on Long Island."[21]

Another prominent example of this type of work is found at the West Angeles Church of God in Christ, the fifteen thousand member church pastored by Bishop Charles E. Blake. Its more than eighty ministries make this church an exemplar of community activism. The most important of these for our purposes is the Community Development Corporation (CDC). Concerned with the promotion of justice, the CDC is responsible for forty-four homes in and around the Crenshaw area of Los Angeles. But beyond the development of actual housing, this corporation provides technological assistance to those interested in various aspects of community development. The CDC's work, which began with a staff of five, has grown to ten full-time employees, fifty volunteers, and a board of directors of more than twenty.[22]

On the other coast, during the 1980s St. John Baptist Church of Miami developed the St. John Community Development Corporation as a way of organizing affordable housing. The process involved both building new structures and revamping existing houses. In addition to the resources of the congregation, St. John, like many other churches, has secured local, state, and federal funds to bring about the revitalization of its neighborhood. As of 1987, the CDC's plans included more than twenty houses as well as the development of commercial property. Other churches are involved in similar projects. For example, Atlanta's famous Wheat Street Church built senior-citizen housing as well as general low-cost homes. In fact, Wheat Street is said to have been one of the first black churches in the country to concentrate on the development of affordable housing when, in 1961, its development corporation used government aid to build an apartment complex on twenty-two acres.[23]

Finally, there is First AME Church of Los Angeles. Its Renaissance Program is funded through a unique relationship with the Walt Disney Corporation, which donated one million dollars to finance the church's micro loan program. As of 1994 the program had distributed roughly $700,000 to black Americans and members of other minority communities.[24]

Most of the black denominations with financial resources have been involved in the development of colleges and seminaries. However, the training offered by these denominationally sponsored institutions of higher learning are only valuable if children graduate from high school. This is a large *if*. Questions persist concerning the adequacy of public education for American children, particularly children of color, who are overly represented in decaying urban schools with poor resources and overburdened teachers. According to some, the proper response is the transformation of these schools through governmental intervention and activism on the local level. Examples of this include various "adopt-a-school" projects through which churches—such as Metropolitan Baptist Church of Washington, D.C., and Apostolic Church of God in Christ of Chicago—take personal responsibility for basic school supplies and tutorial assistance. Similarly, many churches seek to supplement public educational opportunities through Headstart programs and after-school tutorials.

In some cases churches have pooled resources. The Montgomery S.T.E.P. Foundation, housed in the Dexter Avenue King Memorial Church in Montgomery, Alabama, was organized in 1986 to provide tutorial programs in local housing developments and a local elementary school. Its central goal is "to proclaim the gospel of Jesus Christ to the poor by mobilizing the Christian churches in Montgomery, Alabama, to work with the poor and with agencies which help the poor so that people are elevated and poverty eliminated for the glory of God."[25] Another collaborative work approach is Project SPIRIT (Strength, Perseverance, Imagination, Responsibility, Integrity, and Talent), run by a collective of churches in three cities—Oakland, Indianapolis, and Atlanta. Project SPIRIT was founded in 1978 by Bishop John Hurst Adams of the AME Church as a way of organizing the educational activities of several major black denominations (including AME, CME, COGIC, National Baptist Convention of America, and the Progressive National Baptist Convention); it is an offshoot of the Congress of National Black Churches.[26] Through this project students in junior high schools receive assistance with basic writing and math skills. Project SPIRIT serves an important need with respect to "latch-key kids" who would otherwise spend a good number of after-school hours in unsupervised and perhaps harmful activities. The goal is to branch out beyond these three cities, and through its programming increase the number of black children finishing high school and college.[27]

Some churches have developed private educational institutions to control the physical plant as well as the curriculum. Many parents find the cultural and religious sensibilities that inform church-based school curriculum appealing. Notable examples include Allen AME Church's Allen Christian School started in 1986. It provides traditional education (plus religious and cultural elements) for children from pre-kindergarten through junior high school. Other AME churches with low cost, quality educational opportunities for community children include Bethel AME Church of Baltimore and Bridge Street AME Church of Brooklyn. Baptist churches including Concord Baptist Church of Brooklyn also sponsor schools. But beyond this, Concord developed the million dollar "Christfund," through which the church since 1988 has given roughly $80,000 each year to the Billie Holiday Theater for young artists, the Brooklyn Academy of Music, and other community ventures.[28]

The central premise behind these various activities—economic development, housing, and education—is control of neighborhoods. As Rev. Johnny Ray Youngblood and numerous other ministers have noted, a primary command for the church is "thou shalt buy up the neighborhood." The idea behind this is simple. If churches can help community residents control the educational thrust, economic solvency, and residential character (proper housing) of their neighborhoods, they stand a better chance of stopping drug dealers, absentee landlords, and other harmful forces from destroying black lives.

Poverty and Environmental Racism

Writing about her own life, Beverly Hall Lawrence notes:

I equate our rejoining the church with an overt political statement or a nationalist, pro-black act. At the heart . . . of our intentions seemed a suggestion that we were part of a new generation of "believers" seeking to revive the church as an instrument of change. Our generation, it seemed, wanted to return to the historical roots of the church that had been led by our foreparents during each critical stage of racial progress from Emancipation to the movement for civil rights.[29]

For many, political consciousness has revolved around issues of race and racism, the continuing struggle for racial equality. However, a new development in black churches relates political consciousness to the environment and environmental racism. As theologian and Baptist minister Garth Baker-Fletcher argues, black Americans have historically fought for dignity, but they have failed to think in broad terms; they limit this to the quest for *human* dignity. He argues for a rethinking of this to include the dignity of the earth, including consideration of environmental destruction. For many, including Baker-Fletcher, this does not entail ignoring human needs. Rather, environmental destruction and human prejudice are intimately connected. In Baker-Fletcher's words:

> Strong theological censure of human injustice as well as concern for the nonhuman world is needed. Without such censure one suspects that ecological concern could become an abstract exercise of those detached from and unconcerned about genuine human oppression. Expressing moral concern for the nonhuman world without an explicit call for human dignity leads to an inadequate view of dignity.[30]

A more complex sense of dignity and oppression is not a concern limited to academics like Baker-Fletcher; some churches and their leaders also are trying to connect these two concerns, human oppression and environmental destruction, through a critique of environmental racism.

The rationale for this shift is straightforward: the effects of environmental pollution and destruction are felt by the entire global population. From global warming to nuclear waste and toxic spills, unchecked and short-sighted approaches to the natural environment have taken their toll. And although all peoples face these problems, environmental crises have stronger effects in some communities than in others. Ethicist Emilie Townes argues that "sixty percent of the total Black population lives in communities with one or more uncontrolled toxic-waste sites."[31] Environmental activist and organizer Charles Lee argues that many black Americans live near a toxic waste site, and 15 million live close to more than one. What Townes and Lee hint at is the idea of environmental racism, that is, the understanding that socioeconomic conditions premised on racism are a factor in a community's exposure to environmental problems. In the words of author Robert D. Bullard:

This in no way means that some white communities have not been adversely affected by industrial pollution. . . . However, the poisoning of African American communities . . . [is] not as well known to the public. Environmental and health risks are not randomly distributed throughout the population. On close examination of the costs and benefits derived from unpopular environmental decisions, communities of color have borne and continue to bear a disproportionate share of the burden of the nation's pollution problems.[32]

For example, for fifty years, Houston placed many landfills and solid-waste processing plants in black communities. Further north, residents of Chicago's heavily black American South Side face problems generated by waste dumps, factories, and landfills. Black Americans in West Harlem, New York City, live with a major sewage plant, highways, and a station for the collection of garbage.[33] Situations like those in Houston, Chicago, and New York also are faced by black communities in many of the nation's large cities and rural areas.[34] And when efforts are made by black communities to change placement of hazardous waste and industries, lawsuits are not always successful. Sometimes environmentally destructive industry has resulted in job opportunities for some, but with a great cost.

Environmental hazards—whether from pesticides, solid-waste processing, lead poisoning, or other sources—result in health problems. Although there is no consensus on the amount of exposure necessary to cause serious health risks, it is likely that rates of asthma, reproductive problems, cancer, and other life-threatening illness are enhanced for black Americans by exposure to environmental destruction.

The Black Church and the Environment

Although environmental issues have plagued black communities for some time, black denominations have been slow to involve themselves in environmental justice activities. However, interdenominational organizations working on environmental racism have reached out to black churches, and this is beginning to have an effect. According to Harry A. Wheeler, his denomination, the CME Church, has not really worked on issues of environmental destruction, but the "National Council of Churches has made the CME Church aware that this is a problem that we need to address. Thus I have been appointed to the Eco-Justice Working Group and my personal awareness has been heightened."[35] Wheeler speaks in terms of a consciousness-raising taking place in 2000, but cautious involvement on the part of black churches with ecumenical or interdenominational organizations concerned with the environment dates back two decades. For the most part, this involvement has been, as Wheeler's comment suggests, concerned with fact finding or awareness enhancement for black churches. Yet this involvement is important because it marks an attempt to become theologically sensitive to environmental issues by modeling God's creative and nurturing attitude toward life. As an issue of the *AME Church Review* points out:

> There is a biblical vision that can help inspire and support humanity's struggle toward sustainable approaches to the future of ourselves and the planet. The Book of Job makes clear the need to view creation in an holistic manner: "Do you know when the mountain goats give birth? Do you observe the calving of the deer?" To begin to think and act more like God means knowing and loving our landscape. . . . By living sustainably—in ways that are informed, wise, and good—we, as one Indian development worker said, have the joy of recreating the Garden of Eden.[36]

Years earlier, in the 1980s, the United Church of Christ's Commission for Racial Justice, with the participation of many black denominations, began to talk in terms of environmental racism and environmental justice as a way of linking issues of racism with the impact of environmental damage on peoples of color. Connected to this, in 1982 prominent black church figures such as Rev. Joseph Lowery (of SCLC) and Walter Fauntroy (a minister in the Progressive National Baptist Convention) participated in protest against dumping of harmful chemicals in Warren County, North Carolina.[37] Although these leaders gained national headlines, black churchwomen from the area played a major role in protesting the dumping of toxic soil in their community. By the time the protest reached its peak, hundreds of protesters had been arrested as part of the first large-scale arrests for an environmental protest. More recently, in 1991, the commission sponsored a summit—National People of Color Environmental Leadership Summit—in Washington, D.C., during which people from various communities discussed the manner in which environmental destruction of water, land, and air is linked to racism.

This summit drew much of its ideological and theological underpinning from the 1987 report "Report on Race and Toxic Wastes in the United States," issued by the United Church of Christ Commission of Racial Justice and supported by several major black denominations. The summit served as a forum for concerted environmental effort on the part of people of color and, by so doing, it ignited the environmental justice movement, which became the major vehicle for protest against environmental racism. The goal of the summit was to demonstrate that environmental trauma affects all communities and therefore should be a primary concern for all Americans, regardless of color and class. The various communities of color represented at the summit sought to recognize their links and common concerns and to force policymakers to recognize the value of and respect for all peoples. In short, the summit called for a responsible relationship between the earth and all peoples, based on respect and justice.[38] Its "Principles of Environmental Justice" outlined its demands, including "universal protection from nuclear testing, extraction, production and disposal of toxic/hazardous wastes and poisons and nuclear testing that threatens the fundamental right to clean air, land, water and food."[39] Furthermore, the summit called for an end to toxins and other environmentally destructive products, and also demanded that polluters correct the harm done, including full compensation to victims and safe working conditions for all employees.

Through the early 1990s the Black Church's environmental efforts revolved around education and conversation, a recognition of the links between the traditional issues of concern addressed by black churches and the destruction of the natural environment. For example, in 1993, the National Council of Churches in cooperation with the major black denominations (AME Church, AMEZ Church, CME Church, NBC USA, NBCA, PNBC, and the Church of God in Christ) held a summit—National Black Church Environmental and Economic Justice Summit—in Washington, D.C. Drawing on the concept of environmental racism developed during the 1980s, members of this summit—such as Charles G. Adams, pastor of Hartford Memorial Baptist Church (Progressive National Baptist Convention); Bishop Fred James of the AME Church; Bishop Thomas Hoyt, Jr., of the Christian Methodist Episcopal Church; and W. Franklyn Richardson, general secretary of the National Baptist Convention, U.S.A., Inc.—focused on the manner in which toxic waste and other environmental hazards are disproportionately found in communities of color.[40] The basic goal of the summit was to educate black churches concerning environmental justice and to help them develop a plan of action, highlighted by a list of six demands given to former vice president Al Gore by Franklyn Richardson. These included "the naming of a Black Church representative to the Sustainable Communities Task Force of the President's Council on Sustainable Development" and the "involvement of local Black church congregations in major environmental decisions undertaken by the administration."[41] Also important was the declaration on environmental and economic justice resulting from conversations among the various church leaders: "We, African-American

Church leaders, historically committed to justice issues, affirm the unitary nature of life and commit ourselves to the ministry of converging justice and environmental issues that are critical matters of life and death for our Church and for our community."[42] This declaration serves as the central agenda of the Black Church Environmental and Economic Justice Network created during the summit. Acting on this agenda will include establishing a fund to provide seed grants to local congregations working on issues of environmental justice. In addition, on the national level the denominational representatives involved in the summit committed themselves to educating church members on issues of environmental justice and to bringing issues of environmental racism to the attention of governing bodies such as general boards and conventions.

To carry out these goals, denominational leaders agreed to make use of the resource kit (including the "Principles of Environmental Justice" and other materials presented during the summit) developed by the National Council of Churches of Christ and distributed to church leaders, church publications, and church educators. Participation on both the national and local level was envisioned this way:

1. The Black Churches [*sic*] will educate its constituency about legislative and executive initiatives on environmental justice issues. A system of ACTION ALERT mailings will be established to facilitate this task.
2. The Black Churches [*sic*] will strongly encourage teach-ins on environmental injustice and environmental issues in general.
3. Black Church representatives will endeavor to attend environmental meetings sponsored by denominations and activists. The NCCC [National Council of the Churches of Christ] will circulate a list of such up-coming meetings and seek representatives from Black Church leaders.
4. Black Church representatives will participate in the Environmental & Economic Justice Working Group to ensure continual involvement around this issue.
5. Black Churches will, whenever possible, provide a platform for environmental justice activists to tell their stories of local struggle to Black congregations.
6. Black Churches will endeavor to visit sites of environmental degradation which are in cities where they are convening their annual meetings.
7. Black Churches will provide representatives to be involved in the Toxic Tours being organized by the Working Group.

8. Black Churches will explore the feasibility, together with the NCCC, of putting together a Black Church Toxic Tour which will visit some of the sites discussed at the Summit. They will use their influence with the Black pastors in such cities to encourage them to be supportive of local struggles against environmental racism. They will also meet with local corporate heads to express their concern about issues.

9. Black Churches will, together with the NCCC, monitor and follow-up on the six requests made to Vice-President Gore at the Summit.

10. Black Churches will join in the challenge to mainstream environmental organizations to expand their agendas to include justice issues.[43]

Several denominations—AME Church, AME Zion Church, and CME Church—are part of the working group and have selected individuals as coordinators of environmental programming as a way of bridging the gap between denominational concerns and local activities. Although the Baptist conventions have not officially joined the working group, Rev. Dr. Angelic Walker Smith of the National Baptist Convention, U.S.A., Inc., plays a major role in the National Council of Churches and its work on environmental issues.[44] For example, Dr. Walker Smith has worked on both the national and international level to increase awareness of environmental issues effecting communities of color.

The environmental justice program sponsored by the Eco-Justice Working Group serves a major role in the dissemination of information concerning environmental hazards. For example, in 1998, under its sponsorship, a group of representatives from the Church of God in Christ, the AME Church, the Progressive National Baptist Convention, and the African Methodist Episcopal Zion Church toured Louisiana communities that are suffering from toxic contamination. The idea behind the tour was to encourage black churches to become more involved in particular campaigns against the type of environmental racism operating in Louisiana communities such as Convent, Oakville, and New Sarpy. After the tour, representatives from the various black denominations pledged themselves to a meeting with Al Gore to discuss needed improvements, as well as to more concrete efforts within their various denominations to curb environmental racism and its ramifications.

Founded in 1983, the Eco-Justice Working Group holds as its primary concern developing and distributing materials for use in local congregations that help Christians understand their relationship to the earth;

the National Council of Churches' "Web of Creation" website provides the basic message communicated to congregations:

> God created the earth and all that is in it and declared it good. God's creation is marked by wondrous complexity, interdependence and beauty. Human beings are called by God to the task of stewardship—taking care of the earth respectfully for its own sake and so that present and future generations may live on it and enjoy its fruits. The gifts of creation and the responsibility of stewardship were given to all of humanity, so that all might have enough and no one would have more than is needed and God's justice would prevail.[45]

Much of the material available through the group is similar to that which other organizations provide concerning conservation of energy and land, but what differs is the manner in which participation in environmental work is given a religious or faith-based mandate. Drawing from scriptural passages such as Matthew 5:16, the National Council of Churches urges local congregations to become stewards of the environment as part of their Christian conduct. As part of this commitment to God's creation, for example, congregations are encouraged to reduce energy consumption. In order to bring this sense of stewardship to life, individuals and churches can request various programs and packets, such as the "Climate Change Strategy Packet," which provide information on and governmental policy toward climate change. Another program available from the Eco-Justice Working Group is the "Energy Stewardship Congregations Program," through which local congregations adjust their energy consumption as a part of their faith commitment. Congregations and individuals securing this information on energy consumption are provided a list of energy-saving practices, and a form letter that can be filled out and sent to the president as a sign of support for a clean energy agenda for the twenty-first century. The idea is to get congregations involved through information and exposure to environmental issues. So, for example, materials from the Environmental Justice Covenant Congregation Program encourage church leaders to hold activities outdoors and to make use of field trips to areas of environmental damage as a way of showing what happens to the waste humans produce.

Efforts that do not necessarily make use of environmental-racism language include the programs of the National Religious Partnership for the Environment (NRPE). Beginning in 1993, and based on a partnership of four groups (the US Catholic Conference, the National Council of the Churches of Christ, the Coalition on the Environment and Jewish Life, and the Evangelical Environmental Network), the NRPE made available almost 2 million dollars to promote environmental concerns. The organization's goal is clear:

> The Partnership seeks to weave care for God's creation throughout religious life in such a way as to provide inspiration, moral vision, and commitment to social justice for all efforts to protect the natural world and human well-being within it. It calls upon multiple resources to enact a comprehensive vision.[46]

Through the National Council of Churches of Christ, several of the black denominations participate, at least indirectly, in the NRPE's effort to promote a certain vision of effective stewardship of the world.

The Church World Service (CWS), in which all three black Methodist denominations (AME, AMEZ, and CME churches) and all three Baptist conventions (National Baptist Convention, U.S.A., Inc.; National Baptist Convention of America; and the Progressive National Baptist Convention) participate, comprises thirty-five church organizations. The CWS was started after World War II as a way of providing relief materials such as clothing, medicine, and food to needy communities across the globe. It also works to promote "the integrity of the environment" in ways that are not confined to issues of environmental racism.[47]

Denominations that are not listed as members of groups mentioned above have voiced a concern with the environment in other ways. The three major black Baptist conventions, for example, have signed statements to this effect as part of regional Council of Churches organizations. In Pennsylvania, these three shared a concern with waste management stated in this way: "We urge the elimination of the use of non-biodegradable products and the reduction of reliance on industrial processes that generate hazardous waste. . . . We support minimal packaging concepts. We encourage legislation directed towards the useful recycling of waste materials."[48] This statement and others directed at various dimensions of the environmental crisis are framed by a concern that humans adopt lifestyles that recognize the links between all forms of life and God. The stance taken by the churches in Pennsylvania is matched by the work of others, including the Washington [State] Association of Churches, which includes AME and AMEZ congregations. Through partnerships with environmental organizations, community-service groups, and labor unions, the association seeks to serve "as a focal point for dialogue, advocacy, action and reflection." In so doing, its "work is rooted in the conviction that our Christian faith calls us to act with compassion for people and respect the sacredness of life. We feel called to the challenge of unity in our society by addressing the needs of community in our world."[49]

Local Churches on the Environment

On the local level the Eco-Justice Working Group, composed of black and white denominations, provides techniques for increasing environmental awareness. Some of the suggested approaches include placing pertinent materials, such as articles on the environment, in denominational journals, church bulletins, and church newsletters, as well as requesting that local newspapers run similar materials. Congregations are also encouraged to make use of environmental-justice materials in classes for children and adults. Furthermore, the group asks congregations to visit local officials to voice their concern with environmental destruction and their support for environmental justice. Churches interested in less public activities can take advantage of the materials available for congregational development. For example, *Faith-Based Environmental Justice Resources for Youth and Children* lists various resource books, service-learning projects, inspirational stories, and crafts projects that bring children into contact with environmental issues.[50] The goal is to help children think about their personal activities as ways to mirror God's concern for the natural environment.

Other materials offered through the National Council of Churches help local churches think through the Bible with sensitivity to environmental issues. One such resource is *And the Leaves of the Tree Are for the Healing of the Nations* by Carol Johnston of the Christian Theological Seminary. Johnston's book leads local church study groups through an analysis of various portions of scripture such as Genesis 1:1—2:30, which deals with the creation of life, and New Testaments teachings by Christ that speak to his concern with the redemption of all creation. Working through Johnston's text is meant to help Christians rethink their theological commitments in light of a concern for the health of the world. The assumption is that a redefined theology sensitive to environmental issues will result in local church activities that are environmentally sound. In short, the book is meant to help churches develop a better sense of stewardship:

> We set out to find theological foundations for eco-justice—for enacting economic justice in concert with environmental integrity. As Christians, we start with the Bible, to see how nature and economy

fit into the Divine economy of creation and redemption. To our astonishment, what we find is far more than a smattering of relevant texts. From the first chapter of Genesis to the last chapter of Revelation, the biblical witness consistently and frequently affirms God's care for creation and each creature, especially the most vulnerable—both human and non-human. . . . By following the Bible through from beginning to end, then, we can see how eco-justice is not just one more cause in a long string of causes, but the connector in which we human beings can see our proper place and find both liberation and balance through restored trust and communion with God and all our neighbors.[51]

With this sense of stewardship in place, the working group's *101 Ways to Help Save the Earth, With Fifty-two Weeks of Congregational Activities to Save the Earth* provides practical ways for individuals and local churches to implement their heightened sensitivity to environmental concerns. After short explanatory statements concerning major environmental challenges such as ozone depletion and acid rain, the manual provides practical ways of changing individual and congregational lifestyles that serve to improve the environment. Individuals, for instance, are encouraged to reduce electricity consumption, monitor the efficiency of automobiles, and purchase environmentally sensitive products. The manual also provides information concerning recycling opportunities in each state. With respect to congregational activities, a fifty-two week schedule helps congregations shape worship and other events around a concern for the environment. Suggestions for churches include participation in Earth Day activities and serving as a community recycling center.[52]

In addition to the Eco-Justice Working Group, other organizations have developed over the past decade to assist congregations with environmental education. They include the National Religious Partnership for the Environment, the North American Conference on Ecology and Religion, and the North American Conference on Ecology and Religion. Whether drawing from the resources of these national organizations or not, some black churches have developed creative approaches to environmental crisis and environmental racism. First AME Church of Los Angeles, for example, has a water conservation program. In cooperation with the Metropolitan Water District and the Department of Water and Power, the church exchanges old devices such as shower heads and toilets as a way of reducing the amount of water wasted through inadequate equipment. As of a few years ago, the church was responsible for updating approximately one thousand pieces of equipment each week. On both the denominational and local levels black churches have made use of existing resources and theologically based commitment to black America to address issues of economic hardship and environmental destruction. New housing has been developed, and educational opportunities and job training provided. In addition, black churches are beginning to recognize the links between poverty and exposure to ecological damage. And, giving attention to the growing environmental-racism movement, they are beginning to educate black Christians concerning the importance of linking economic progress to concern for the environment.

5

The Black Church
on Health and Sexuality

The economic problems addressed by black churches have wide-ranging implications with respect to the overall quality of life experienced by black Americans. One of the most telling areas revolves around health and health care. The gains made by black Americans over the course of the past three decades have not necessarily translated into better quality of life with respect to health and resources for effectively managing health issues. What activist and college professor Angela Davis notes concerning the health of black women is applicable across the black community. She writes: "In this society, dominated as it is by the profit-seeking ventures of monopoly corporations, health has been callously transformed into a commodity—a commodity that those with means are able to afford, but that is too often entirely beyond the reach of others."[1] Health care has become an industry, viewed as an enterprise with primary concern for profit as opposed to treatment; this means that those without financial resources receive limited care. According to Emilie Townes, a social ethicist writing on health care, "people who earn less than $9,000 a year have the highest death rates and are more likely to have hypertension, arthritis, upper respiratory illnesses, speech difficulties, and eye disease."[2] The official desegregation of health care held benefits for black Americans in that, in theory, it increased access to the nation's health-care infrastructure, but the benefits were in reality limited. Historian Edward Beardsley speaks to this point: "Increased professional care was only the most obvious determinant of health and arguably not the crucial one. As always, non-medical variables—lifestyle, nutrition, education, racism and especially economic status—had an influence too, not just on blacks' need for care but also on their ability to act on that need and to profit from whatever professional contact did occur."[3] The health concerns Beardsley notes are extremely important and have been for some time, but in the following pages attention is given to two health issues that have had a staggering impact on black Americans' health during the past several decades: illicit drugs and HIV/AIDS.

Illicit Drugs

Taking the United States as a generic whole, the 1970s marked a major increase in drug use and trafficking. According to estimates, between 1970 and 1975 seizures of cocaine by U.S. agents increased by 700 percent, and in 1978 three tons of cocaine were confiscated.[4] Although problematic, use of cocaine was not extremely large scale in black communities until the introduction of "crack" in the 1980s. This drug provided a quick and relatively inexpensive high, but with the same dangerous health consequences.[5] The demand for this product and the money that could be made from it resulted in a new economy within many communities as some street gangs and other interested parties turned to drug dealing. With this explosion in the crack cocaine market came violent turf wars between groups pushing for greater areas of distribution. A consequence of this sub-economy of illegal activity was a tremendous increase in the number of young men in prison on drug-related charges as well as an increase in violent crime and the homicide rate for men below the age of thirty.

Tragic in and of itself, this situation is made more severe because of the effect of cocaine and crack on the unborn. As of the late 1980s it was estimated that more than 10 percent of all children born in the United States were prenatally introduced to drugs, including cocaine. For these children withdrawal is a minor difficulty compared to the serious birth defects and long-term developmental consequences associated with their exposure.[6] The onslaught of crack cocaine has resulted in other forms of strain on both immediate and extended families as well as communities.

HIV/AIDS

First recognized early in the 1980s, HIV/AIDS has had devastating consequences. While debates raged concerning the best way to discuss, describe, and medically address HIV/AIDS, the virus's toll on human life continued to grow. According to the U.S. Department of Health and Human Services, as of 1989, less than a decade after the first reports of AIDS, almost 30 percent of all AIDS patients had contracted the disease through shared needles. The same report indicates that at the end of the 1980s, a primary means of introducing the HIV/AIDS virus into the larger, heterosexual population was through sexual contact with drug users. Furthermore, most children with AIDS were exposed before birth through a drug-using parent, and the number of reported cases of infection nationwide has experienced rapid growth in part because of the number of children infected.[7]

Although blacks do not constitute in actual numbers the bulk of those suffering with HIV/AIDS, the rate of infection is frightening. "Blacks constitute 37 percent of all those who contracted AIDS through needles and 48 percent of those who contracted AIDS through partners who used dirty needles. These patterns of transmission largely explain why blacks are 27 percent of all people with AIDS, and black women are 52 percent of all women with AIDS." Black men are almost three times as likely as white men to contract AIDS, and black women are twelve times as likely as white women.[8]

The Black Church, Health, and Health Care

With respect to the two areas of concern here—illicit drugs and HIV/AIDS—the collective Black Church's activism is often associated with the work of spokespersons such as Rev. Jesse Jackson and organizations such as the National Conference on the Black Family/Community and Crack Cocaine. Using these two as examples, the Black Church has typically but not exclusively responded in two ways: (1) slogans, and (2) distribution of information and suggested policy reform. One of the best examples of slogans is Rev. Jackson's "Down with Dope! Up with Hope!" Such slogans were intended to motivate black Americans to take control of their communities and personal dealings. They were a moral charge given to adults and young people to own themselves with respect to health issues. In the words of Rev. Jackson: "Our total community must reject the dope pushers and see them as terrorists. We must change our minds, our morals and our conduct."[9] Many denominations and their local churches adopted this approach, using catchy slogans in the pulpit and youth programs as a way of inspiring children to avoid drugs. This motivational technique at times has been combined with a more direct attack on the relationship between drug flow into communities and the U.S. government. Again drawing from Rev. Jackson:

> Until the American people responded to our campaign message of "Stopping Drugs From Flowing In and Jobs From Flowing Out," Nancy Reagan was just saying *"No!,"* Vice-President and Republican Nominee George Bush was *just saying nothing*, and President Ronald Reagin was *just doing nothing*—except cutting the Coast Guard's drug interdiction budget by $100 million while international drug trafficking was increasing.[10]

In addition to the work of individuals like Jackson, the Congress of National Black Churches has been involved in health-care issues, particularly drug abuse. Its primary involvement has centered on assistance and training programs through its national anti-drug and violence campaigns. The goal of this work is increasing public awareness of drug abuse and subsequent violence and developing strategies—in conjunction with churches, government agencies, and community activists—whereby residents of troubled neighborhoods can combat drug distribution and use. As of 2000, these campaigns were taking place in thirty-seven cities, with almost 2,000 members of the clergy, and an impact on an estimated 500,000 people through funding of over 13 million dollars.[11]

The National Conference on the Black Family/Community and Crack Cocaine held in 1989 involved twelve hundred churches from a variety of denominations and health care professionals. One of its activities was the development of a framework to help black churches across the country collectively orchestrate anti-drug use programs and activities. The major emphasis of these nationally coordinated activities revolves around the constructive use of free time, assuming that many children become involved in distributing and/or using drugs—including crack—because of few outlets for the positive use of time and inadequate employment opportunities. This initial conference spawned other conferences and strategies for ending illicit drug use in black communities. In South Carolina, for example, an effort known as Project ADAM—Anti-Drug Abuse Movement—brought together one hundred black churches for the purpose of public education on drug abuse. Recent ADAM activities have included walkathons in numerous cities and youth clubs to provide productive outlets for free time.[12]

Many regional church councils are also involved in the anti-drug campaign across denominational lines. In Pennsylvania several of the major black denominations joined forces with other churches in the development of a position that is worth briefly presenting here. They argued concern for the health of the larger community is biblically mandated and must be the business of the contemporary churches. Beyond this, the churches must serve as the moral compass with respect to medical ethics related to technological advances. This direct work, however, must be combined with pressure on the federal government.

> While affirming this tradition of health care by church-affiliated institutions, we recognize that health-care costs are prohibitive. We believe government must play an important role to assure that all people, regardless of the ability to pay, will have access to adequate health care. This care should truly be holistic health care, geared to the prevention of illness and the maintenance of health.[13]

The Black Church's commitment to dealing with illicit drugs is evident in word and deed. However, the HIV/AIDS epidemic has not been as unilaterally addressed. Silence on this issue is often considered appropriate because many black Christians entertain conspiracy theories related to HIV/AIDS that promote suspicion concerning the disease and the medical industry's research and treatment efforts. According to some accounts, this disease entails a governmentally engineered plot to remove undesirable populations, notably homosexuals, drug users, and racial minorities. The appeal of conspiracy theories, however, is not without some merit when one is mindful that earlier this century black men infected with syphilis remained untreated in order to study the effects of the disease on the human body and mind. (This experiment took place at Tuskegee University and is called the Tuskegee Study.) Therefore the government and the science industry are capable of horrific deeds in the name of "medical advancement." But is HIV/AIDS another example of this? Rev. Ronald J. Weatherford puts the issue in perspective. He says in a recent issues of the AME Church's *Christian Recorder*: "While white power structures are to blame for the conspiracies of medical experimentation, neglect, racism, and politics, the African American community is behind the conspiracy of silence. For years, black leaders ignored AIDS, regarding it as someone else's fight. Like lepers, African American families affected by AIDS bore the shame and burden alone."[14]

Beyond conspiracy theories, for some churches HIV/AIDS is theologically problematic, particularly in light of the rather faulty ontology of AIDS fixed on sexual conduct embraced by most. It is assumed by many black Christians that God's involvement in the world as outlined in scripture extends to the area of health, and this includes the spread and cure of various illnesses. As Reverend Robinson of the African Methodist Episcopal Church notes:

> For the faith community, the question still centers around the agency of that disease. Why did it appear? Was it sent? Why is there no cure? Why is it uniformly fatal? Why are we seemingly powerless over it? Why does God allow it to continue unchecked? What does it mean? These are questions of theology and theodicy, power, will, purpose and providence, and even ego. Undoubtedly, these are questions of tremendous complexity; for AIDS presents one of the most complicated interrelationships between potentially conflicting theological constructs: our theologies of disease, faith and healing; our theologies of lifestyle and personal responsibility; and our theologies of sin and salvation.[15]

As Rev. Robinson suggests, the issue is not really one of grand conspiracies but rather of a certain perspective on sexual relations in light of scripture and church tradition. Ruby Bailey, a writer for the *Detroit Free Press*, cuts to the quick:

> Two of the three easiest ways to contract HIV are among the most prominent sins in the Bible—extramarital sex and gay sex. Churches balked at passing out HIV-prevention pamphlets that promote the use of condoms rather than abstinence, because they said that following such pamphlets compromised their Christian values. Christ, after all, they said, healed the sick but also said, "Go, and sin no more."[16]

Others question AIDS education because they do not want to give the impression that they condone premarital sex. One gets a hint of this in the following statement offered by the AME Church with respect to HIV/AIDS. In this statement it is argued that the Church must "take an uncompromising stand for abstinence from premarital sexual activity, balanced with a commitment to addressing the issues in people's lives (particularly the lives of our young people) that lead them to resort to high risk behavior such as sexual promiscuity."[17]

More progressive and less scripturally literal Christians recognize that black churches have an obligation to serve their communities and address cases of AIDS, recognizing that the sufferers are individuals, real people, in need of compassion. Turning again to Reverend Robinson:

We have to invoke a kind of theological casuistry, dealing with AIDS on a case-by-case basis. There will always be individual scenarios, invoking very different theological constructs. We may never understand. Understanding, in this life, is not promised. We may never be able to reconcile the divergent messages, and our diverse opinions, with the diversified scriptures. . . . We may never understand. Understanding is not promised. But, in the meantime, perhaps we can all agree and covenant to do as Jesus did. . . . We can covenant to have compassion.[18]

This does not mean a surrender of moral and ethical commitments, but it does mean an attempt to suspend judgment and to focus on human need. Black churches through the Pennsylvania Council of Churches, for example, echo this perspective: "We ask that public and private resources be appropriated for AIDS prevention, for adequate care for AIDS patients on a continuing basis, and for research toward a cure for the disease."[19]

The Pennsylvania Council of Churches' stance hints at a move away from a theological interpretation of disease as sin, and this is one of the most progressive developments in church circles during the past two decades. When considered a form of sin, it is more likely that churches will provide spiritual resolutions that often do not move beyond the level of prayer. On a pragmatic level, in making this move it becomes easier for the Black Church to secure funding from secular organizations to support programs because the request for support is not so grounded in theological concepts. This is not to say that the Black Church has or should forsake its theological/spiritual sensibilities; rather it is a matter of combining the two.

Realizing that the Black Church needs assistance (such as technical infrastructures) in developing programs related to AIDS, Pernessa C. Seele developed an organization named Balm in Gilead. She says:

There is no doubt that the link between HIV/AIDS, drug abuse and sexual activity has been a stumbling block for churches who feel that such behavior is contrary to their tenets. Fortunately, increasing numbers of churches are realizing that providing AIDS education and social services is consistent with the teachings of Jesus Christ. Clearly, Jesus' actions on behalf of the sick show us how we should behave during this age of AIDS.[20]

Supported by all the major black denominations, Seele's group provides education as a preventive measure as well as services to those infected.

Among the projects developed by Balm in Gilead is the Black Church HIV/AIDS National Technical Assistance Center. Guided by groups of experts and monitored by the Columbia University School of Public Health, the center serves as an information clearinghouse for those seeking information on HIV/AIDS and funding for service-related programs. This educational thrust will be broadened to include the development of Sunday School materials for children, but for now it provides churches with information related to four areas: (1) AIDS, spirituality and the Black Church; (2) the Church's role in HIV prevention; (3) developing sermons on HIV/AIDS; and (4) facts about AIDS and African Americans.[21] In addition, the organization draws on the worship-related dimension of the Black Church tradition by supporting a Black Church Week of Prayer, encompassing some five thousand churches, with the focus being on the request for divine intervention and human compassion. Started in 1989 in Harlem, this week of prayer has taken place eleven times in various locations.[22] The goal is simple:

> The Black Church Week of Prayer for the Healing of AIDS is a week of education and AIDS awareness that spotlights the role that churches are playing in addressing the AIDS crisis. Each year, a growing number of churches within Black communities are developing AIDS prevention outreach programs, supporting and caring for persons living with HIV and establishing HIV testing facilities complete with counselors knowledgeable about HIV/AIDS and spiritual care.[23]

Seele's work has inspired others to become involved. The Harlem Congregations for Community Improvement Corporation, for example, is composed of ninety churches in New York. First started in 1985, this organization, founded by Rev. Preston Washington of Memorial Baptist Church, devotes most of its resources to HIV/AIDS education and prevention. Projects include a two million dollar housing project for families dealing with the virus, an information resource center, and a support network that provides information to other religious organizations interested in AIDS ministry.[24]

Health Care on the Congregational Level

It is clear that many local churches are working to address some of the health-care problems facing black Americans. Efforts with respect to general health care typically fit into three categories: (1) medical assistance,

(2) information and education, and (3) prevention programs. Some churches with major resources, such as Rev. Otis Moss, Jr.'s, Olivet Institutional Baptist Church of Cleveland, have recognized the inadequacy of overcrowded emergency rooms in county hospitals and are seeking to remedy this through the construction of alternate hospitals. Olivet, in 1998, developed the Otis Moss, Jr., University Hospitals Medical Center in cooperation with University Hospitals of Cleveland. It is staffed by seven doctors, two nurses, and four medical assistants. Whereas the medical treatment offered is in keeping with traditional practices, this hospital overtly promotes a link between the body and spirit. According to Pastor Moss: "There's no true separation between body and spirit. . . . And when there's an attempt to separate the two, something suffers."[25] This church and its pastor are not alone in rethinking black health care through the creation of alternate sites of assistance. The East Brooklyn Congregations (EBC), led by Rev. Johnny Ray Youngblood and mentioned in an earlier chapter, is a collective of fifty churches that not only develops affordable housing but also builds health-care facilities in East Brooklyn. For example, St. Peter Claver provides medical treatment for the uninsured. Whereas most churches cannot afford such grand approaches to health care, they often use members who are medical professionals to provide checks on blood pressure, and so forth. Furthermore, it is not uncommon to find announcements in church bulletins related to the availability and importance of these services. Some churches, in addition to providing direct services, have made connections with local agencies and agents and attempt to help their communities through referrals to health-care professionals. Beyond this, churches on the local level also attempt to prevent illness through various programs such as exercise nights geared toward adult members of the church. With respect to children, many local churches sponsor sports teams as a way of keeping children active. This prevents some of the problems associated with unsupervised time and promotes good health through physical activity.

Beyond general health care, many black churches give primary attention to preventing drug use through contact with children. For example, during the 1980s First AME Church of Los Angeles developed an annual meeting with two thousand at-risk children, who were given moral and values-related information. At the end of this annual event, the children were urged to sign commitment letters vowing to remain drug free and gang free for ninety days. Some churches have targeted alternative employment options as a way of keeping young people off drugs. The rationale is simple: If young people have rewarding forms of employment they will be less likely to use or distribute drugs. A continuation and expansion of this "safe space" concept is found in the work done by Allen AME Church of Queens, New York. Recognizing that children within some of the worst sections of the church's neighborhood needed a space in which they were safe from the dangers of the streets, Rev. Flake developed in 1992 the Shekinah Youth Chapel. Encouraging some of Allen's young people to transfer to this new chapel, and with Rev. Anthony Nathaniel Lucas in charge, they begin mentoring young people in the neighborhood. Within its first six years the membership of the chapel had grown to five hundred, most being new members from the community. Such growth entails numerous lives changed, children moving from crime and drug dealing to a church-centered existence. According to one young man: "Pastor Lucas meets with me one-on-one and says, 'Right now, let it go. Put it all on Christ and let it go.' . . . Our church in Queens, not the streets, is our home. . . . All of a sudden, I'm struggling to see how I can help him reach other kids on the streets."[26] Hartford Memorial Baptist Church in Detroit makes use of a similar strategy, but with a job-skills component. In cooperation with the local council of Baptist pastors the church developed a program in auto mechanics.[27] The idea is to provide skills resulting in meaningful employment as well as information concerning drug abuse.

While these prevention programs are popular and useful, some churches undertake intervention programs through which drug addicts are encouraged to change their behavior. St. Stephen's Church of God in Christ located in San Diego has a program through which recovering drug users spend evenings out in the community in conversation with drug dealers and abusers, using their personal experiences as a way of encouraging others to make the same move. This is part of the church's social-service program provided through its ministry of reconciliation. George D. McKinney, the church's founder and pastor, has this to say about this dimension of the church's work:

> As the neighborhood became predominately a black neighborhood, certain racial and economic and social problems which are intensified in the black community emerged. . . . The church became a center and a meeting house where people of good will, both black and white, joined in a constructive effort of understanding and dealing with these problems. Thus, the church attempted to show concern for the whole man and to become involved totally in his situation.[28]

With respect to HIV/AIDS many black churches seek to assist those who have contracted the disease through attention to the basic matters of life. For example, church members will help with preparation of meals, house cleaning, and maintenance of medicine schedules. In some instances churches also maintain support programs such as housing and testing services. The goal, however, is not simply to comfort those who are infected, it is also a matter of preventing the spread of AIDS. Churches interested in moving in this direction are given assistance by organizations such as Rosalind Worthy's Gospel Against AIDS, which seeks to bring churches, social-service agencies, and victims of AIDS into conversation as a way of better addressing the disease's impact on black communities. The effect of this organization is small because securing volunteer AIDS workers from the churches has been difficult, but the potential is extraordinarily large. Finally, seminary professor and AME Church minister the late Annie Ruth Powell developed a program that operated out of her apartment. Called the Christian Community Learning Center (CCLC), it began offering health-care information and ministry in 1990. According to Powell:

> This ministry offers cancer and AIDS-related education, as well as education on family violence. The objective here is to address human need on a physical, emotional, and spiritual level and join the struggle against disease and violence. Partnerships with other agencies permit CCLC to participate in clergy-training on health issues as well as provide education for church and community.

Powell became sensitive to the need for additional information on health care because of her personal battle with breast cancer. In going through treatment she found that many survivors "relied heavily on their faith in God not only for physical healing, but for emotional and spiritual healing and the strength to endure when death was imminent. Therefore the kind of assistance the church can and should give must not be minimized."[29]

Once churches recognize the importance of their involvement, they begin to develop approaches to the problem, including testing programs, published literature, counseling, and in some cases housing. West Angeles Church of God in Christ provides some of these services through its Counseling Center, which includes an AIDS support group geared toward "the restoration and edification of the psychological, emotional and spiritual health of individuals, couples, families, and groups through a Christian perspective."[30] On the opposite coast, in Boston, several black churches have teamed up to address the issue of HIV/AIDS through an organization called Who Touched Me Ministry. Participating churches, including Charles Street AME Church, Columbus AME Zion Church, and Little Zion Church of God in Christ, train church members to provide current information on the virus—its causes, treatments, and impact on black communities.[31] In extremely rare cases, with churches such as First AME Church, part of the prevention work involves distributing condoms. Some black Christians object to this practice because they believe it entails the church endorsing sex outside marriage and, from their reading of scripture, this is sin. Nonetheless, more daring churches believe saving lives is the first priority.

Sexuality and Homophobia

Few issues across denominations have been handled as badly as that of sexuality. Philosopher Cornel West speaks about the "missing in action" status of major black institutions, including the Church, when saying that "these grand yet flawed black institutions refused to engage one fundamental issue: black sexuality. Instead, they ran from it like the plague. And they obsessively condemned those places where black sexuality was flaunted: the streets, the clubs, and the dance-halls."[32] Defining an acceptable and working standard of black Christian sexual identity has been difficult. On one hand, the black body and black sexuality were ignored or rejected by the larger society. On the other hand, efforts to critique and move beyond this negative assessment entailed for many a celebration of the black body and sexuality. Could the Black Church, mindful of Christian tradition on sex and sexuality, embrace this celebratory posture?

As ethicist Kelly Brown Douglas demonstrates in much of her recent work, all too often the Black Church has attempted to cover sexuality with religious platitudes. According to cultural critic and Baptist minister Michael Dyson, "To a large extent, the black church has aimed to rid the black body of lascivious desires and to purge its erotic imagination with 'clean' thoughts."[33] This is often played out with respect to "proper" dress and presentation as well as restrictions on activities that are considered acceptable. For example, some of the more fundamentalist black denominations discourage members from attending movies and listening to secular music because they believe they bring sexual urges and desires to the surface. Few churches fight through this to offer informative and insightful sex education and counseling for its members. Even fewer do so in a way that recognizes talk of abstinence alone will not solve problems such as teenage pregnancy. Sex is discussed in less than helpful ways by too many youth ministers who respond to queries about sexual activity with a cute but empty response: "You can do anything

you feel comfortable doing *with Jesus standing next to you.*" Even conversations that extend beyond this simplistic approach tend to offer a
"say no" policy without great attention to sexual urges as a natural
component of our humanity. That is to say, the blanket "just say no"
policy does not help young church members understand their sexual
urges. An example of this limited response is given by a minister who
says:

> In addition to providing our young men options other than the
> penal system, we must tackle the problem of teenage pregnancy.
> Our young women must learn to treat their bodies like the temples
> they are. Having a baby is not cool; it is a serious responsibility
> that requires financial security, maturity, and a lot of patience. I
> challenge our youngsters to realize and understand that having a
> child is not synonymous with your manhood or womanhood. We
> must teach our young women that they should not fall prey to peer
> pressure.[34]

Such statements may satisfy the sensibilities and sexual mores of some,
but what exactly do they mean? What practical consequences are connected to the energetic articulation of such mantras?

To avoid the discomfort of explicit conversation on sex that recognizes humans as sexual beings, many churches limit themselves to discussions of manhood and womanhood—masculinity and femininity—as
a way of preparing young men and women for their scripturally defined
responsibilities and socially prescribed relationships within the context
of the traditional family. It seems logical that the Black Church and its
various denominations would give a great deal of attention to issues of
manhood and womanhood when one considers that black Americans
for centuries were questioned on these grounds. They were represented
in the popular imagination as menacing black bodies that posed a threat
to the quality of life for white Americans. The structure of the slavery
institution and the requirement for total control on the part of slave
owners resulted in African males exercising none of the responsibilities
traditionally associated with adulthood and masculinity: they did not
control their own bodies, relationships, and had little say with respect to
the inner workings of their families. After slavery, black Americans continued to be questioned regarding socially accepted standards of femininity and masculinity. In short, the sexuality of black Americans
remained a problem for white Americans, one they dealt with through
stereotypes and at times violence. In the late twentieth century studies

such as the Moynihan Report of 1965—"The Negro Family in America: The Case for National Action"—lamented a "pathology" associated with black family structure. Subsequent interpretations of these studies tended to center on males, with some theorists arguing that the "damaged" structure of the black family resulted in an inability to train properly young black boys toward manhood. Others suggested the racism present within the United States is the real problem preventing many black males from forging productive and rewarding lives and relationships. Whatever the case, there remained a risk to being black and male in the United States. For example, the high homicide rate, the high rate of incarceration for black men, combined with unemployment problems and the decline in the number of black men entering higher education all point to a problem.[35]

Influenced by these studies and current statistics concerning the "endangered" black male, the Black Church has understood the demise of black communities in large part as the demise of black men and has tackled this problem by presenting itself as friendly toward strong notions of masculinity. This has meant addressing stereotypical depictions of men involved in the Church:

> The image of Christ is "wimpish" and encourages black men to "turn the other cheek" in response to racial injustice; that the traditions of "blond and blue-eyed" images of Christ reflect blacks' self-hatred and capitulation to white supremacy; that religious services are too emotionally driven because the churches are dominated by women, who "by nature" are emotional; and that, unlike the Nation of Islam, which among many unchurched men represents the essence of black manhood, black churches attract homosexuals.[36]

Churches such as Bethel AME Church of Baltimore are trying to counter this perception of Christianity as "soft" by depictions of a muscular gospel geared toward men. At Bethel, church member Goldie Phillips puts it this way:

> Under Pastor Reid's charge, they cannot look at Christianity as sissified. . . . If they belong to this church and they've been studying under him for any time, impossible to view it like that [*sic*]. The brothers who come to church, they need to be touched, I mean physically touched. They need to know that they can maintain their macho manhood, but they can be touched.[37]

This attempt to portray Christianity as a man's religion might increase the number of men, but it promotes in the process a nasty homophobia and heterosexism supposedly grounded in the Bible.[38] Scripture cited to support homophobia and heterosexism is drawn from both the Hebrew scriptures (Old Testament) and the Christian scriptures (New Testament). For example, according to the book of Genesis, in the beginning, God created man and woman and put them in relationship with no sanction of same-sex intimate relationships. And, for more explicit attention to the subject many black Christians point to Leviticus: "Thou shalt not lie with mankind, as with womankind: it is abomination" (18:22) and "If a man also lie with mankind . . . they shall surely be put to death" (20:13). And, in the Epistle to the Romans, Paul makes this statement:

> For this cause God gave them up unto vile affections: for even their women did change the natural use into that which is against nature: And likewise also the men, leaving the natural use of the woman, burned in their lust one toward another; men with men working that which is unseemly, and receiving in themselves that recompense of their error which was meet. (Rom 1:26-27)

In its most counterproductive stance, the Black Church joins other religious organizations in condemning homosexuality. Even when many black Christians in the Black Church seek to be liberal and understanding, their perspective still smells of homophobia. For example, it is common to hear members of the Black Church say with confidence: "We must hate the sin [homosexuality] but love the sinner." Phrased this way, the problem remains the same, just couched in a comfortable silence. When not met with silence, a kind of "I won't ask and don't you say," lesbians and homosexuals within the context of the Black Church are often condemned and/or ordered in sermons to save themselves from themselves. What Bishop William A. Hilliard of the AME Zion Church said concerning his denomination holds true for many others: "The Church is diametrically opposed to homosexuality; we stated that as our official position last year at our national conference, it is a sin."[39] At its worse, the Black Church has acted with hostility toward homosexuals, blaming them for their own victimization. The paradox and hypocrisy of this position escapes many black congregations whose "machismo" oppresses a segment of the black population and forces many to implicitly (if not explicitly) reject loved one, neighbors, and co-workers.

Although many churches have softened their position, at least rhetorically, it can still be difficult for openly gay individuals to obtain ordination, for example. This has been the case for Tommie Watkins, an openly gay man seeking ordination in the AME Church. Watkins leads a ministry for gay and lesbians at Greater Bethel AME Church (Fort Lauderdale, Florida). Watkins was not ordained, although he had completed the Church's required program of training. The reason recently offered by Bishop John Hurst Adams is this: "The church position is clear. If a person is openly practicing homosexuality, we are unlikely to ordain them [*sic*], because [homosexuality] is not consistent with creation; it's not consistent with Scripture and the church."[40] Adam's perspective is in keeping with the perspective of the denomination that made this statement during its 1976 General Conference:

> As a church we categorically, unreservedly and unequivocally reject the concept of homosexual marriage as being totally inconsistent with the biblical and theological conceptualization of marriage as viewed and practiced in our Zion. . . . As interpreted by our theology, the Bible makes no provision for a married relationship between two persons of the same sex. We, therefore, expect our ordained ministry to reserve the rite of marriage for those of different sexes. We expressly forbid our ministers to extend the marriage rites to homosexuals or to two persons of the same sex. As a church we do not recommend the homosexual lifestyle to our constituency.[41]

Not all AME ministers agree with this position, but until the church hierarchy in this denomination and others like it changes its attitude, the heterosexist perspective will continue, and gay and lesbian ministers will need to hide their sexuality in order to pursue ordained ministry.

There are, however, venues through which homosexuality is tolerated by the Church. For example, black churches make little of homosexuals in choirs or serving as choir directors. In speaking about his development in the Black Church, Cornel West provides a prime example of this.

> I know when I was growing up in the black community, most people knew that, let's say, the brother who played the organ in the church was a gay brother. People would say, oh, that's so-and-so's child. You know, he's that way. And they'd just keep moving. There wasn't an attempt to focus on his sexuality; he was an integral part of the community. It wasn't a matter of trying to target him and somehow pester him or openly, publicly degrade him. Those who said he's "that way" didn't believe that way was desirable, but they just figured that's just the way he was, that's just his thing, you know.[42]

Some might "accept" a homosexual choir director or member as long as the person maintains a low profile. This "acceptance," however, is often passive aggressive. In the words of Rev. Yvette Flunder: "We sing their songs and shout and get happy off their music, but condemn them privately."[43] A gay man involved in the Black Church provides an example of this:

> I really see a persistent problem in the church. . . . I'm now sixty and I've been working in the church since I was ten years old. And the issue of sex, this business of homosexuality, has been wrapped in hypocrisy for too many years. Because even when I was a kid of ten, twelve when I first started playing piano, I used to hear ministers say they were going to find them a real sissy to play music in their church. . . . So while on one side of the pulpit the picture was condemning sex between people of the same sex, on the other side in order to enhance and build their congregation and get the people shouting they were willing to forget the so-called theological issues in order to enhance their pocketbook, so you know. The hypocrisy must be addressed.[44]

This testimony speaks to an implicit mandate that black gay and lesbian laity and ministers must deny—at least in public settings—an element of their identity. As problematic as this is, it is so deeply seated that it usually goes unnoticed. Baptist minister and academic Michael Dyson points this out by giving attention to a common scenario within Black Church worship. He writes:

> A black minister will preach a sermon railing against sexual ills, especially homosexuality. At the close of the sermon, a soloist, who everybody knows is gay, will rise to perform a moving number, as the preacher extends an invitation to visitors to join the church. The soloist is, in effect, being asked to sing, and to sign, his theological death sentence. His presence at the end of such a sermon symbolizes a silent endorsement of the preacher's message. Ironically, the presence of his gay Christian body at the highest moment of worship also negates the preacher's attempt to censure his presence, to erase his body, to deny his legitimacy as a child of God. . . . The black church, an institution that has been at the heart of black emancipation, refuses to unlock the oppressive closet for gays and lesbians.[45]

What results from this perspective and resulting activities is a form of heterosexism. That is to say, the same scriptural rationale used to condemn homosexuality is also used to buttress heterosexism, because in condemning homosexuality, the argument goes, God sanctioned heterosexuality as the only proper form of sexual relationship. The Black Church is a victim of this perspective, speaking in liberating terms only with respect to socially sanctioned modes of sexuality and gender dynamics. Thus the Black Church through its doctrine fosters a world in which only heterosexual contact is appropriate, and by this the Church entrenches itself in the mainstream at the expense of many members of the black community it actually seeks to protect. In this sense the Church participates in the construction of a restrictive and dangerous society. In the words of gay-identified, bisexual theologian Elias Farajaje-Jones:

> In the minds of most people, our lives do not exist apart from sexual acts. Most people are not aware of the fact that many queers are barred from access to housing and to certain forms of employment. We are often at risk losing our jobs if it is discovered that we are queer. If we have children, they may be taken from us. Certain insurance companies will not insure us because we are perceived as more at risk for HIV than other people. As queers, we exist as criminals in most states where there are anti-sodomy laws, laws based on a heterosexist, homophobic/biphobic interpretation of Genesis 19:1-10.[16]

The Black Church's Response

Organizations such as the Religious Coalition for Reproductive Choice (RCRC) and its Black Church Initiative recognize the importance of the Church in the life of the black community and are working on ways to help improve its ability and willingness to talk about sexuality. On July 8-10, 1998, RCRC sponsored the National Black Religious Summit II on the Howard University School of Divinity campus. This meeting gathered together four hundred clergy, church laity, educators, and young people—representing almost half the United States—to talk about sex and sexuality. Carlton W. Veazey, president of the RCRC, summed up the summit's mission this way: "We no longer feel intimidated by the forces that would have us remain silent about sexuality. The black church has come to understand that we must minister to the whole person, not just a person's spiritual life but every part of his or her being, recognizing the interrelation of our sexual nature and our spiritual nature."[47] The summit was part of a larger agenda including a clearinghouse of information for use by churches as well as curriculum and forums focused on preparing ministers for regional summit activities. A primary and ongoing objective of the Black Church Initiative is multi-week educational programs for church members, both youth—the "Keeping It Real" curriculum—and adults—the "Breaking the Silence" curriculum.[48] The former is a seven-week program geared to teenagers. Meeting in small groups with a facilitator, issues such as teen pregnancy are addressed through role playing, readings, attention to popular culture, and scripture. The objective is to provide teens with tools and information necessary to make wise sex-related decisions. For most churches participating in this program, the first option is abstinence, but the program affords an opportunity to talk about safe sex and other issues through seven topical discussions: "Sex and Sexuality: A Spiritual Gift from God"; "It's a Family Affair: The Role of Family in Understanding Ourselves as Sexual Beings"; "Sexual Identity: How and When Do I Express Myself as a Sexual Being"; "The Impact of Peer and Societal Pressure: The Role and Influence of the Media"; "The Influence of the Church"; "The Freedom to Choose: Life Choices Related to Sex and Sexuality"; and "The Tension Between Freedom and Responsibility: The Impact on the Whole Person." To prepare for these meetings, facilitators are given a packet containing resources—such as information from the National Campaign to Prevent Teen Pregnancy—and activity books.[49]

The goal of the adult curriculum is to prepare parents and church leaders to address issues of sex and sexuality with young people. The "Breaking the Silence" curriculum is not meant to predetermine answers to pressing sexuality questions; rather, the intent is to prepare adults to help children make wise and healthy decisions. Using the same methods—role playing, and so on—adults address three major areas: "Circumstances and Sexuality"; "Choices and Sexuality"; and "Consequences and Sexuality."[50] It is difficult to say exactly how many churches are using these materials, but it is safe to say that black denominations remain behind the learning curve with respect to sex and sexuality.

On the seminary level, United Theological Seminary in Dayton, Ohio, with assistance from the RCRC, has recognized the need for attention to this issue and is planning to offer a program entitled "Spirituality and Sexuality in the African American Church." Seminary project fellows involved in the program will participate in discussions concerning sexuality and will write a thesis containing ideas to be implemented within their local church settings. Beyond working within a particular church, graduates of the seminary program also work with the RCRC for three years. It is this last element—implementation—that represents the project's primary contribution to the training of clergy. With their training, seminarians are in the best position to help churches rethink doctrine. Some have tackled this by arguing that scripture used to condemn homosexuality was developed in a particular cultural and historical context and this context contained elements of patriarchy and homophobia. Furthermore, Jesus speaks out against many forms of sin, but homosexuality is not listed as sin anywhere in his recorded words. Such being the case, it is not doctrinally mandatory that the Church condemn homosexuality as sin.

Over the past few years various organizations have stepped up efforts to educate the Black Church—its laity, ministers, and professional thinkers—about the homophobia and heterosexism that mark its history. Examples of this include "Racism, Sexism, and Homophobia in Our Time: United We Stand," a public forum held on July 23, 2000, in Miami, Florida. Sponsored by the National Religious Leadership Roundtable and convened by the National Gay and Lesbian Task Force (NGLTF) Policy Institute and Equal Partners in Faith, this session took place at Greater Bethel AME Church and presented talks by Greater Bethel's pastor and the executive director of NGLTF. A few months after this meeting the Kelly Miller Smith Institute on the African American Church and the Carpenter Program in Religion, Gender, and Sexuality, housed on the campus of Vanderbilt University Divinity School, sponsored a conference entitled "The Black Church and Human Sexuality." Participants, including academics and ministers from various denominations, conversed on three primary areas: (1) the deconstruction of sexuality, (2) the Bible and sexuality, and (3) teaching/preaching about sexuality. The goal of both events was to forge new relationships and enhance knowledge concerning pressing issues. These efforts are important because information and conversation may improve the Black Church's sensitivity to and work regarding important issues such as homophobia and heterosexism.

Local Churches on Sexuality

An emphasis on the development of men along traditional ideals of masculinity and manhood seems to be the dominant work on sexuality on both the denominational and local levels. In countless congregations across the country programs are being developed that attempt to socialize young boys. For example, West Angeles Church of God in Christ has developed a discipleship program in which youngsters are matched with older men and, during both structured activities and more informal time together, the older men teach these youngsters how to be "men." The rationale is that many young black males grow up in families without a strong male role model, and they need external assistance in defining their proper role within family structures and society at large. The assumption, of course, is that these young men are heterosexual and will some day develop traditional nuclear families.

Some churches have made use of the Promise Keepers and similar movements to define manhood and the responsibilities of men. Beginning in 1991, the evangelical Promise Keeper meetings have grown from fewer than five thousand in attendance at rallies to over 1 million in 1996.[51] Many black men found the Promise Keepers "promising" in that gatherings often entailed a commitment—sadly enough it proved only rhetorical—on the part of those gathered to improve race relations as a part of a commitment to Christ and to strengthen families and other relationships along traditional lines of male/female authority.[52] Thus the Promise Keepers allowed black men to think in terms of male responsibility and family structure in ways that bring them into the norm. Beyond the Promise Keepers some black churches have also involved themselves with the Moral Majority. For example, according to James S. Tinney, prominent church leaders such as Joseph H. Jackson of the National Baptist Convention, U.S.A., Inc., and the late J. O. Patterson of the Church of God in Christ at least gave the impression of support for this organization.[53] The interest of black males in regenerative activity was further marked by the presence of approximately 1 million black men in Washington, D.C., during Minister Louis Farrakhan's 1995 Million Man March. During this event black men recommitted to spirituality and proper conduct with respect to themselves and their families. The intent of Promise Keepers, the Million Man March, and other events of rediscovery is to bring men back into the center of both spiritual and social existence. At best they are claiming responsibility for misdeeds, but at worst they are reasserting male dominance—and heterosexism—in religious guise.

Although church work related to homophobia and heterosexism lags behind the effort made with respect to issues of economic justice and health care, some local churches are attempting to change this. For example, Greater Bethel AME Church of Florida, mentioned earlier, has developed various outreach programs meant to address gays and lesbians as a neglected segment of the Black Church population. Along this line, hosting the NGLTF conference is just one way in which Greater Bethel seeks to bring attention to the often violent homophobia within our country and the ways in which the Church can work to end this abuse and discrimination. The work at Greater Bethel started roughly five years ago, when Rev. Marilyn Ushers, one of the church's ministers, was made aware that blacks from the church's neighborhood of Overtown were going elsewhere for prayer and guidance because they did not believe black pastors in the Overtown area were sensitive to their issues.

According to Ushers, "They feel isolated and would really like to be able to come to their pastor to talk about it, their sexuality." Greater Bethel began developing programs geared toward promoting this conversation.[54]

It is likely that issues of sex and sexuality will remain difficult for the Black Church and its various local congregations into the immediate future. However, it is also safe to say that addressing these issues must become a priority if the Church is to maintain credibility. To maintain a positive public image, it must treat all its members with fairness and compassion. Continuing the Church's trend toward growth from the 1990s into the twenty-first century requires a much greater sensitivity to and respect for a full range of life options and choices.

6

Sexism and Church Ministry

The activism described in previous chapters would be impossible without the assistance and support of black women, who make up roughly 60-70 percent of the Church's membership. In the words of Baptist scholar Helen Gray: "Visit many Black churches on a Sunday morning and most of the pews are filled with women. Long considered the backbone of the Black church, women account for the majority of the membership and often serve as their congregations' fund-raisers and mission workers."[1] Yet, one of the most widely debated concerns during the entire history of the Black Church, an issue cutting across all denominations, is the role of women within Black Church life and activities. Each denomination has tackled this question in light of its rules and regulations, but the response has been similar regardless of disciplinary distinctions. In part this results from a common perception of gender roles and socially defined notions of womanhood that have guided the Black Church as well as the larger public.

During the antebellum period a Victorian ethos developed called the cult of true womanhood, which argued that the proper role for women was in the home, nurturing the family. Furthermore, women were to be submissive to men and work to ensure the morality of all those within their home. According to historian Paula Giddings:

> The true woman's exclusive role was as homemaker, mother, housewife, and family tutor of the social and moral graces. Isolated within the home, women "raised" men above lusty temptation while keeping themselves beyond its rapacious grasp. Women's imprisonment in the home virtually guaranteed piety and purity. Submissiveness, too, was assured where housewives depended on male support.[2]

Although economic necessity did not always allow such "leisure," it was understood, particularly within southern culture, that white women should have no duties outside the home; even the task of taking care of the domestic sphere was, when financially feasible, left to black women and black children. Clearly black women were not placed on a pedestal; rather, they were worked hard like men, physically abused by white women, and sexually assaulted by white men who, with great absurdity, accused them of provoking passion and thereby "forcing" sexual relations.

The push to develop strong black families once slavery ended included an attempt to forge clear distinctions between "manhood" and "womanhood"—masculinity and femininity—with respect to social activities, family responsibilities, and when possible, work. Blacks made an effort to mirror what they saw in the larger society with respect to gender roles, but economic hardship and social discrimination made this difficult at best. Yet the effort was persistent and advocated by most black civic leaders. The domesticity thesis squarely differentiated private and public, and it placed black women squarely in the home while giving black men control over political issues and other large (public) life altering questions. Major black institutions, like the Church, supported this patriarchal perspective, asserting with biblical certainty that women must in all instances obey the authority of men, both in secular and sacred matters. This attitude, however, did not prevent women from exercising some authority, if not autonomy, in two primary spheres: auxiliary work and ordained ministry.

Black Women and Auxiliary Work

From maintaining the church's records—membership, financial, weekly bulletins, and so on—to caring for the physical plant, preparing the items necessary for worship (communion elements and aesthetic effects such as altar coverings), providing religious education through Sunday school and vacation bible schools, developing and administering congregational clubs and activities such as pastor's aid societies, and fund-raising, women enable churches to maintain their public presence. In recognition of their importance to the Church's longevity, some churches in the twentieth century made an effort to place women on traditionally male dominated boards. For example, Emma Dillard was made a trustee at Concord Baptist Church in New York in 1935, and Lucille Brooks Taylor served as a trustee at First AME Zion Church in 1942.[3] Yet most women exercise power and influence on church activities through boards and clubs designed exclusively for women. Accordingly, "in those denominations in which women were unable to become elders, pastors, and bishops, they assumed the roles of church mothers, evangelists, missionaries . . . deaconesses . . . these alternatives were also available in those denominations in which women were eligible for all leadership roles. When church women were officially 'the second sex', they achieved quite powerful positions of influence and structural authority."[4] Their numbers, consequent resources, and auxiliary positions allowed black women to develop what historian Clarence Taylor calls "parallel leadership" or what sociologist Cheryl Townsend Gilkes refers to as "soft" authority.

Deaconess and Stewardess

Within Methodist churches the position of deaconess was developed as a non-ordained form of ministry for women during the nineteenth century. Although the current function of a deaconess and the number of women holding this position within denominational limits are highly dependent on the personality of each particular pastor, there are several functions that seem less influenced by congregational differences. A deaconess is generally recognized as an advisor to the pastor of the church, helping to maintain the church's growth and direction. In addition, the deaconess plays a major role in carrying out the community service of the church through attention to the homeless, the poor, the elderly, and others in need. In so doing, she helps to maintain healthy relations between the church and the larger community. To be considered for the office, a woman must be a widow or unmarried. When selected, a deaconess is consecrated by the bishop. Methodist organizational structure also includes the stewardess, who makes preparations for baptism and communion. She maintains garments and coverings used on the altar and baptismal pool as well as helps in others ways deemed necessary by the pastor. Although stewardesses are not necessarily older women, they are "mature" both socially and spiritually. Younger women are placed on the junior stewardess board in order to train for work as a stewardess.

Deaconesses in Baptist churches assume responsibilities that in most cases blend those held by Methodist deaconesses and stewardesses. They are responsible for maintaining the materials necessary for the church's sacraments, and they also conduct a good deal of the church's outreach by caring for the needy who approach the church for assistance and by nurturing new church members.

Deaconesses in the Church of God in Christ perform similar functions to those in Methodist and Baptist churches. They are church "helpers" who, among other things, have responsibility for the care of ritual items and spaces.

Church Mothers

Despite typically circumscribed functions performed by deaconesses and stewardesses, women have exercised a degree of control through influence and persuasion, and one of the best examples is the church mother. This is a title bestowed upon older, wise, and spiritually strong women who have distinguished themselves through service in numerous capacities. Once a woman receives this title, she achieves new status based on moral and spiritual authority. Within many churches church mothers determine, for example, what is considered proper conduct for young people outside the church walls ("Representatives of Jesus don't go to worldly dances," or "Would you wear that style of clothing if Jesus were visible in the room?"). Beyond determining external conduct, church mothers are also consulted with respect to the spiritual direction of the church: Should the order of service be changed? What types of paintings should be hung in the church? Cheryl Townsend Gilkes discusses their role:

> Occasionally, the church mother performs the role of a stage manager or director of public worship. Where tension exists concerning

certain practices, her opinion may prevail. In one Baptist congregation, the insistence by the church mother that "this is not a Sanctified Church!" moved the deacon board to call an emergency meeting
with the pastor in order to persuade him to withdraw his permission for drums to be used during the morning service: the church
mother prevailed. Other members of the congregation may walk
out when they disagree with the pastor, but their actions will be
ignored. The church mother is never ignored.[5]

While strong within black Baptist and Methodist churches, the church
mother's implicit authority is even stronger within the Church of God in
Christ. This, however, does not fundamentally disrupt the male-centered
core of the denomination because church mothers give primary attention to educating and "training" women. In other cases their authority
is felt, for example, with respect to the church's selection of pastoral
leadership; a church mother's support for a particular candidate may
result in him receiving the appointment, or this support can help a candidate navigate his way through the ordination process with fewer difficulties. Furthermore, in many cases obtaining a license as an evangelist
requires the approval of both the pastor and the church mother, as indicated by both signatures on the license.[6]

Women as Ordained Ministers

The number of black women in ministerial positions in the Black
Church is not proportional to their presence in the Church's overall
membership. They represent only approximately 5 percent of the combined clergy in the denominations discussed here. Obviously women
within the Black Church exercise their preaching interests primarily
through non-ordained positions. Their function in these roles dates to
the early years of the Black Church and accounts for much of the Black
Church's outreach during the early, formative years. Women's missionary societies, developed in part to harness the ministry aspirations of
women, secured financial resources necessary for church expansion. In
many cases women from these societies served as missionaries both on
domestic and international fields.

Other women exercised their preaching abilities as evangelists under
the authority and instructions of a church's pastor. As Baptist scholar
Helen T. Gray writes:

Women wield power in missionary societies and auxiliaries, and they
maintain active ministries as musicians, speakers and educators. His-

torically denied recognition as preachers, they have accepted such titles as exhorters, evangelists and missionaries—and they've preached anyway. Some have preached without licenses within their denominations; others have chosen to launch independent churches.[7]

Dissatisfaction with the opportunities afforded missionaries and evangelists has led some to fight prohibitions on preaching by challenging the traditional reading of scripture's injunction against women in church leadership positions. The Apostle Paul's comments on such restrictions are measured against the overwhelming ethos of equality that pervades the teachings of Jesus Christ. Also of importance to their argument is the primary role played by women in Jesus' ministry. The work of his mother; the woman at the well, who was commissioned by Jesus to preach; the women who remained with him during his crucifixion while the male disciples fled; the women who first encountered his empty tomb and proclaimed his resurrection—all these make clear the centrality of women to Christ's ministry.

Women Preachers in the Methodist Churches

One of the first to challenge the male-centered mode of operating was Jarena Lee of New Jersey. Born in 1783, Lee experienced a religious conversion after a period of intense angst. Recounting the service, during which the words of Richard Allen stirred her to conversion, she writes in her autobiography, published in 1836:

> I did leap to my feet, and declare that God, for Christ's sake, had pardoned the sins of my soul. Great was the ecstasy of my mind, for I felt that not only the sin of malice was pardoned, but all other sins were swept away together. That day was the first when my heart had believed, and my tongue had made confession unto salvation. . . . For a few moments I had power to exhort sinners, and to tell of the wonders and of the goodness of him who had clothed me with his salvation.[8]

Time would prove that, for Lee, salvation and sanctification were a process rather than a quick event. They would come accompanied by a call to ministry that she shared with Richard Allen. The leader of the AME Church responded that there was nothing in the *Book of Discipline* that sanctioned the ordination of women as preachers. The call to preach, according to Lee, was a gift from God, a matter of inspiration that did not require skills or abilities restricted to men. God can call anyone to ministry. Lee writes:

O how careful ought we to be, lest through our by-laws of church government and discipline, we bring into disrepute even the word of life. For as unseemly as it may appear now-a-days for a woman to preach, it should be remembered that nothing is impossible with God. And why should it be thought impossible, heterodox, or improper, for a woman to preach? Seeing the Savior died for the woman as well as the man.[9]

Wrestling with this call for an additional eight years, Lee recounts a particular worship service during which she was overcome by God's persistent call. In telling readers about this event, Lee reinforces her philosophy of ministry, in which one's call and ability to preach have a metaphysical basis as opposed to training and gender. She writes:

During the exhortation [by Richard Allen] God made manifest his power in a manner sufficient to show the world that I was called to labour according to my ability, and the grace given unto me. . . . I now sat down, scarcely knowing what I had done, being frightened. I imagined, that for this indecorum, as I feared it might be called, I should be expelled from the church. But instead of this, the Bishop rose up in the assembly, and related that I had called upon him eight years before . . . but that he now as much believed that I was called to the work, as any of the preachers present.[10]

Lee was never ordained, although Allen granted her permission to function as an unlicensed exhorter to conduct prayer meetings. Sophie Murray, Elizabeth Cole, Amanda Berry Smith, and other women—were caught by this male-only policy and, like Lee, exercised their call to preach through activities as traveling evangelists and exhorters.

As early as 1844 male ministers began requesting a change in regulations. The best these early discussions could muster was recognition in 1868 of exhorters and evangelists as official offices of church ministry. This was an important step, because it recognized the growing pressure to address a nagging inequality. Still, it was basically an empty gesture because these positions had no real authority; they served as a "glass ceiling" for women but a "stepping stone" or temporary training ground for men. Noting the shallow nature of this alteration did not amount to action against it until 1884, when the AME General Conference agreed to formally license female evangelists, thereby placing them in a category similar to that of local preachers. In 1885 Henry McNeal Turner pushed this process even further by ordaining Sarah Ann Hughes an itinerant (or traveling) preacher, only to have the ordination overturned in 1887. The following year, during the General Conference, bishops were forbidden to ordain women. It was not until 1948 that the church recognized ministry by women as proper through the ordination of Rebecca M. Glover as a deacon. This was an important step, but women in ordained ministry continued to face discrimination with respect to promotion to high levels of authority. For example, even now few women hold important presiding elderships or pastorates of leading churches.

While the AME Church argued with Bishop Turner over the ordination of Hughes, the AME Zion Church was preparing to change its policy permanently. In 1894 Bishop James Walker Hood ordained Julia A. Foote a deacon (and the following year Bishop Alexander Walters ordained Mary J. Small). A quick note on the ministry of Julia Foote is helpful here, because it provides a useful contrast to the experiences of Jarena Lee and others in the AME Church. In so doing, it sets basic parameters regarding black Methodist arguments for and against women in ministry.

Julia A. Foote, born in 1823, exemplified a sensitivity to Christian principles of conduct from a young age. Yet it was not until her fifteenth year that Foote was converted. During a quarterly meeting of her church, the preacher's sermon brought to her attention the troubled state of her soul and the need for a resolution. With an inner turmoil similar to that experienced by Jarena Lee, Foote recounts that she

> fell to the floor, unconscious, and was carried home. Several remained with me all night, singing and praying. I did not recognize any one, but seemed to be walking in the dark, followed by some one who kept saying, "Such a sinner as you are can never sing that new song." . . . In great terror I cried: "Lord, have mercy on me, a poor sinner!" The voice which had been crying in my ears ceased at once, and a ray of light flashed across my eyes, accompanied by a sound of far distant singing. . . . Thus was I wonderfully saved from eternal burning.[11]

As is typical in conversion narratives, Foote feels doubt concerning her experience of God but fights through these periods of uncertainty and works to bring others into a "saving knowledge" of God.

After marrying and moving to Boston, Foote became involved in the AME Zion Church. Her activities ultimately resulted in a felt call to preach that was particularly difficult for Foote because she had up to this point thought of preaching as the domain of men. Foote believed that a resolution had to come or she would lose her sanity, and she resolved to

> do anything or go anywhere for God, if it were made plain to me. He took me at my word, and sent the angel again with this message:

"You have I chosen to go in my name and warn the people of their sins." I bowed my head and said, "I will go, Lord."[12]

Foote's doubts over this calling were magnified by the resistance of many within her church, including the pastor, Mr. Beman. His opposition was not simply to her preaching from the pulpit, it was also a rejection of the holiness-influenced doctrine she embraced. Undaunted by this, Foote preached in her home and in any other venue open to her, even when preaching meant dismissal from her home church. Her persistence and success as a preacher eventually resulted in her ordination as a deacon, followed by ordination as an elder with all the rights and responsibilities that the position entailed.

The CME Church was six years behind the AME Church in ordaining women into ministry, finally ordaining a woman deacon in 1954. While this date is what one finds in most sources, Bettye Collier-Thomas's detailed study of women in ministry notes that the CME Church began ordaining women as local ministers in 1948 and offered full clergy rights to women in 1966. It was in this year, 1966, that Virgie Amanda Jackson Ghant was ordained an elder.[13] Although the CME Church might have taken its cue from the other black Methodists, it is correct to note, as do historians C. Eric Lincoln and Lawrence Mamiya, that the church developed fifty-four years after the AME Church and under different circumstances. This differing historical context possibly influenced the time frame that determined the rise of questions related to ministry. That is to say, the impact of the social gospel and other issues that served as an impetus for the formation of Baptist conventions and the agenda of the other Methodist denominations did not have the same meaning for the CME Church. It was not until the push for women's rights and civil rights during the mid-twentieth century that the CME Church felt compelled to address its own idiosyncrasies.

Having secured ordination in all three denominations, many women now serve as pastors. During the 1980s these included Rev. Christen Stimpson, who pastored St. Mark's CME Church in Springfield, Massachusetts; Rev. Elizabeth Doles, at Martin Chapel AME Zion Church in Mt. Clemens, Michigan; and Rev. Carolyn Tyler, who pastored First AME Church in Indio, California. During the 1990s the list expanded to include hundreds of women in Methodist pulpits around the country. But it remains unlikely that women pastoring churches will be promoted to major pulpits. As AME Zion Church minister Joan Speaks notes: "There are many women pastoring, but in smaller churches. . . . Some women start little churches in their homes. Others just work in churches without pay."[14] Furthermore, it is not uncommon for there to be initial resistance to women as pastors, although their abilities often overcome this. In the words of one AME congregant: "I was one of the ones who didn't want a woman to come here and I was one of the ones who said I would leave the church before I would let a woman be my pastor, and I take it all back."[15] For many women, success as a pastor entails avoiding an overt attack on traditional thoughts about women in the pulpit. Instead, they concentrate on how they fulfill the requirements of the pastorate irrespective of gender: "I don't try to explain myself," says one pastor, "or to justify who I am or to explain what God did when he called me to preach. My whole ministry outlook is to provide a message of hope to a hurting community."[16]

Other women work as chaplains and as assistant ministers in local churches. It is difficult to measure the activities of women operating as chaplains. However, as assistant ministers within local churches, women typically participate in the order of service by delivering sermons, reading scripture during services, and so on. In addition, they often counsel church members on various issues and take responsibility for leading Bible study sessions as well as providing some supervision for church auxiliaries. Although these are typical functions, each church pastor shapes the actual role played by ordained ministers on that person's ministerial staff. In some cases women are ordained for service in a particular church—"local orders"—and serve as the pastor of this congregation. However, as noted above, these tend to be smaller churches or missions with few members and limited resources.

There are several women in all three denominations who serve as presiding elders, the second-highest-ranking position in Methodism. Those holding this position are responsible for the oversight of churches within a geographic region, and they report directly to the bishop responsible for the district of which their region (or conference) is a part. The highest position within Methodism and the one with the most authority is that of bishop. Over the course of the past several decades women running for this office have received more internal church press. Women and some male supporters have pushed for a female bishop for decades, and it finally occurred in the AME Church with the elevation of Vashti Murphy McKenzie to the bishopric in 2000.[17] Bishop McKenzie's stature in Methodism was solidified long before her election when she was assigned by Bishop Brookins to a major pulpit in the AME Church after less than a decade as an ordained minister. As pastor of the Payne Memorial Church in Baltimore, she held a position of denominational authority based on her skills as both preacher and administrator, increasing the church's membership to well over seventeen hundred. Many hope this move on the part of the AME Church will provide a model applied in the other Methodist denominations. Jacquelyn Grant, a theologian and an ordained minister in the AME Church, speaks to this issue:

> Some years ago, my four-year-old niece said to me "you can't be a preacher"; "Why?" I asked. "'Cause you wear ear rings." For her, the wearing of ear rings was a significant public symbol of femaleness. Because the doors to church leadership were open on a very limited basis to women, girls/women lacked sufficient models to encourage them in their journey of life. A model helps to instill confidence in the observer of the model. Its absence does not mean that it ought not be, it means only that it has not yet been a reality. It is not a fail safe means of determining leadership. It simply gives females an opportunity to know that it has been done and it can (and ought) be done again.[18]

Women Preaching in the Baptist Church?

The situation shaping the struggle for ordination in the above churches pales in comparison to the rigid stance taken by most Baptist churches. Because of the loose affiliation marking the three conventions, the debate is primarily addressed on the local and regional levels, with no official Baptist policy. Drawing on scripture, advocates of the "woman's limited role" philosophy point to a divine sanction for their bias: "I am so glad, dear brothers, that you have been remembering and doing everything I taught you. But there is one matter I want to remind you about: that a wife is responsible to her husband, her husband is responsible to Christ, and Christ is responsible to God" (1 Cor 11:2-3, *The Living Bible*). Furthermore, for some, the mere fact that God came to the earth in the form of a man—Jesus Christ—is proof positive that men represent the best examples of God's work in human affairs.

Whereas women typically do not hold pastorates, much of their activity occurs through the Woman's Convention (WC). Formed in 1900 through the efforts of prominent figures such as Nannie Helen Burroughs, this division drew on the energy of regional women's conventions (first developed in the 1880s) and made its goal ministry to the world outside the church. Leaders of the WC did not preach per se, but they gave speeches and lectures across the country in which they outlined a plan for the betterment of the world through high moral and ethical standards drawn from the wisdom of Christian scripture. For instance, Ella Eugene Whitfield labored as a missionary and field secretary for the National Baptist Convention during the early twentieth century and became known for her lectures. Men within the convention such as Rev. Samuel W. Bacote recognized her talents and spoke of her as "a woman of untiring zeal and commanding appearance. She can hold an audience indefinitely, by the intensity of her earnestness and the clearness and appropriateness of her well-chosen words. The utility of her subjects and the excellence of her delivery have rendered her extremely popular as a public speaker."[19] In keeping with early theories of advancement through a form of social conformity, the WC sought to bring black Americans in line with accepted patterns of conduct and aesthetic sensibilities. To accomplish this, the WC operated in accordance with a version of the social gospel that promoted the development of institutions such as schools and settlement houses. The individual responsibility implied here was connected to a recognition of racial oppression but gave little attention to gender roles. Even touted speakers like Ella Eugene Whitfield maintained the status quo with respect to the work of women. In a 1926 sermon she says:

> Mothers, you ought not to go out so much night, stay home and see after your children and see that they prepare their lessons. The school teachers cannot learn them, they must learn themselves. Put fasteners on your children's clothes. I know you go out to work every day, but take the time you have and succeed. The Lord will provide. Wake up, there is danger on the line. Much is being done to destroy homes and happiness. What is meant by the words, Wake up? Study, prepare for service, so you can serve. Put prayer in your homes and bible reading. Try to get along with people. Avoid difficulties. Get your husbands and sons not to drink moonshine. Bathe up and clean up on their work and they will receive more respect. Have pride in the home. The home is the foundation of every life.[20]

Auxiliaries, departments, and the WC have played a major role in setting and pushing the agenda of women within Baptist circles. They have amounted to a force with national and international scope and influence. Yet they do not represent the only avenues for leadership. To the contrary, the strong autonomy of local congregations in decision-making as well as the relative autonomy of regional conventions has resulted in some women being recognized as preachers and pastors. Furthermore, C. Eric Lincoln and Lawrence Mamiya point out, after the death of the pastor, the congregation may vote to have the wife—who has demonstrated leadership and preaching ability—assume control of the congregation. In addition, they note that the Progressive National Baptist Convention has the most liberal stance concerning women in preaching ministry and includes several women on its official roll.[21]

In recent years cracks have developed in the male dominated hierarchal structure, but the general consensus remains against women in ordained ministry. In some instances women serve as assistant pastors and associate pastors, but one might raise questions concerning the "pastoral" duties assigned these women. The president of the National Baptist Convention, U.S.A., Inc., several years ago expressed appreciation for this trend toward women as assistant pastors. Yet, this convention, like the others, has not made an official statement concerning the ordination of women. Still, in spite of resistance several women have made impressive strides with respect to ordained ministry. For example, Rev. Trudie Trimm, pastor of New Testament Baptist Church in Chicago, took over in 1965 the church she and her husband founded and has almost tripled its membership. Overcoming opposition from many ministers, she became the first ordained female minister recognized by the National Baptist Convention, U.S.A., Inc. Her success has required what some might consider an unfortunate compromise with tradition. She does not, as she says, "take the man's ego away from him. I let my 30 deacons lead a lot of the meetings and I sit with the laymen. My ministry is the dictation of the Holy Spirit. My people don't see male or female when they see me; they see a representation of God."[22]

In the Progressive National Baptist Convention one can point to Rev. D. L. Pearson, who was ordained in 1967 and pastors Mt. Olive Baptist Church in Columbia, South Carolina, as another example of the shifting perspective on women in Baptist ministry. These are only a sampling of the growing number of black women representing the changing face of pastoral ministry. The number is even more impressive when one takes into consideration women like Suzan Johnson Cook, who served on President Bill Clinton's National Advisory Board on Race and who pastors the Bronx Christian Fellowship Church, which is part of the American Baptist Convention and the National Baptist Convention, U.S.A., Inc. She has been involved in ministry for some twenty years and has had her share of questions concerning the legitimacy of her "calling." In her words:

> Some men felt threatened initially, and so they would be very resentful in some public places. They would always ask me, "Defend your call. Tell me how you know you were called to preach." And I'd say "Tell me how you know. I mean, that's your issue. You're a pastor; I'm a pastor." And my thing was I was not going to spend my time trying to defend my call, but I was going to spend my time and energy building up the ministry that God has given me.[23]

Progress has been slow, but Baptist leaders such as Franklyn Richardson of the National Baptist Convention, U.S.A., Inc., believe an increased role for women is inevitable: "Ultimately, I think the predominance of women in the church will cause all ministers to realize that discrimination against women cannot continue."[24]

Proclaiming God's Word in COGIC

Within Pentecostal circles one can find women who have founded and/or serve as pastors of churches. Keep in mind that William Seymour's introduction to holiness in California took place through an invitation to pastor a small church that had been founded by Mrs. Josephine Washburn and J. M. Roberts, and pastored by Mrs. Julie Hutchins. Before reaching California he encountered Mrs. Alma White, who founded the Pillar of Fire organization in Colorado. To this list one can add Elder Ida Robinson, who founded Mt. Sinai Holy Church and became the first black woman bishop in the United States.[25] Holiness and Pentecostal churches were always more accepting of women preachers than their counterparts. These women "were somewhat more successful than Baptist and Methodist women in gaining access to the pulpit or lectern" and even "in those churches where they failed, the 'double pulpit' emerged as a compromise between the women's spiritual militancy and biblical patriarchy. In some cases, Baptist and Methodist women defected to the Sanctified Church in order to exercise their gifts."[26] Drawing on scripture, Pentecostal churches recognized preaching ability as defined by spiritual anointing as opposed to gender. Yet, contrary to the above examples and theological rationale, most Pentecostal churches restrict women to non-ordained roles. While recognizing their talents, the Church of God in Christ made the following declaration in 1973:

> The Church of God in Christ recognizes the scriptural importance of women in the Christian ministry (Matthew 28:1; Mark 16:1; Luke 24:1; John 20:1); the first at the tomb on the morning of Christ's resurrection; the first to whom the Lord appeared (Matthew 28:9; Mark 16:9; John 20:14); the first to announce the fact of the resurrection to the chosen disciples (Luke 29:9; 10:22) etc. But nowhere can we find a mandate to ordain women to be an Elder, Bishop, or Pastor. Women may teach the gospel to others (Philippians 4:3; Titus 2:3-5; Joel 2:28), have charge of a church in the absence of its Pastor, if the Pastor so wishes, (Roman 16:1-5) without adopting the title of Elder, Reverend, Bishop or Pastor. Paul styled the women who labored with him as servants or helpers, not Elders, Bishops, or Pastors. Therefore the Church of God in Christ cannot accept the following scriptures as a mandate to ordain women preachers: Joel 2:28; Galatians 3:28-29; Matthew 28:9-11.[27]

Restrictions on ordination, however, have not prevented women within the COGIC from spreading the gospel through teaching ministries, evangelism and more recently through limited access to positions as chaplains.

Regardless of the official denouncement of ordination for women, there are a few examples of women exercising pastoral responsibilities. One prominent example is Rev. Addie Wyatt, co-pastor of Vernon Park Church of God in Christ in Chicago, who was included in the "Honor Roll" of great black women preachers published by *Ebony Magazine* in 1997.[28]

Until women are ordained, if this ever occurs, avenues similar to those utilized in Baptist Conventions are the major source of leadership opportunities for COGIC women. Bishop Charles Mason, founder of the Church of God in Christ, recognized the need for religious leadership outlets. To address this, Mason recruited Lizzie Woods Roberson, previously affiliated with the Baptist church, to create the Women's Department. In this capacity she traveled the country organizing and nurturing the talents of COGIC women and putting in place regional leaders and overseers. Like the Women's Convention discussed above, the Women's Department of the COGIC serves a major function with respect to both spiritual growth (for example, through Bible study and prayer bands) and material development (for example, through an emphasis on education and other aspects of racial uplift). In fact, the denomination recognized the importance of this department to the overall life of the church by labeling its various functions official forms of ministry. On one level, this can be read as a way of pacifying churchwomen while maintaining the church's gender bias. Another way of reading this is to recognize the manner in which it bespeaks the pressure placed on traditional structures of the church while highlighting at least a subtle recognition of the importance to the church of women's financial and structural contributions. But even framed in this way, the controversy over ordination remains a weighty issue. The Women's Department, albeit a recognized power within the denomination, has a limited range of authority in that it sets and organizes the activities of *only* the church's women.

The Future of Women in Ministry

The debate over women in ministry continues in all denominations. In some instances it revolves around opportunities for promotion to the position of bishop or general officer, and in others it entails basic recognition as authentic ministers. It is unlikely that the pressure to address these issues will dissipate any time soon. And this is for good reason: the continuing large number of women in black churches combined with the massive increase in the number of seminary-trained women across the various denominations creates a tremendous paradox and surplus of talent.

As pressure from men and women continues, black denominations will need to ease hard-line opinions or face the loss of membership. For example, the more liberal opinions of the Episcopal and United Methodist churches may entice some women to leave historically black denominations in order to advance their ministerial interests. Or some women may leave historically black denominations and join nondenominational churches that have fewer sexist regulations.

Womanist Theology and the Critique of Sexism

Beginning in the 1970s and moving through the present, scholars such as Jacquelyn Grant, Katie Cannon, and Delores Williams have raised questions concerning the Black Church's stance against racism but relative silence on issues of sexism. Racism is an evil that must be eradicated, but oppression is weblike in nature and therefore, they argue, sexism within the black community must also be addressed. Being Christlike requires a strong response to all forms of evil and to the extent that the Church has failed to address its sexism, it has failed to be Christian. As Jacquelyn Grant stated in 1979:

If the liberation of women in not proclaimed, the church's proclamation cannot be about divine liberation. If the church does not share in the liberation struggle of Black women, its liberation struggle is not authentic. If women are oppressed, the church cannot possibly be a "visible manifestation that the gospel is a reality"—for the gospel cannot be real in that context. One can see the contradictions between the church's language or proclamation of liberation and its action by looking both at the status of Black women in the church as laity and Black women in the ordained ministry of the church.[29]

It was not until the early 1980s that this critique of both the lived Black Church and the study of this Church was given a name that clearly defined its orientation and concerns. Drawing from the work of Alice Walker, Katie Cannon (1985) and Delores Williams (1987) used the term *womanist* to describe the centrality of black women's lives to the formation of their theological perspective. The self-assuredness, self-respect, importance and value of black women and their experience captured by Walker's term spoke to the importance of women's historical presence in the Church and provided the raw material for rethinking how we think and talk about the Black Christian Tradition.

Naturally, there has been debate among black women concerning the proper focus of this theological enterprise—questions of method and theory for the most part—but the concern of revitalizing the Black Church has remained central. Academics exposed the ways in which the Black Church, in the words of Williams, tended to promote teachings that were so "spiritualized and 'heavenly directed' that women parishioners are not encouraged to concentrate on their lives in this world and to fight for their own survival, liberation and productive quality of life. They are not encouraged to develop a self-concept and build female self-esteem."[30] That is to say, although black churches promoted liberation with respect to issues of race and racism, they failed to be as forward thinking when it came to the needs of women within the pews. Ethicist Katie Cannon notes: "We need to analyze the social organization of the Black Church—curricula, music, leadership, expectation, pastor-member interactions—as well as outright sex discrimination. Far too often, the organization of the church mirrors male dominance in the society and normalizes it in the eyes of both female and male parishioners."[31] To correct for this, womanist theologians write, lecture, and preach about the contributions of women to the religious life of the black community. They recall the achievements of early pioneers, like political activists Sojourner Truth and Ida B. Wells-Barnett, and they use these women as examples of how change can be forced upon the reluctant. It is in essence a shift away from male-centered understandings of religious activism, with the intent of empowering women in contemporary black churches to use their history and their numbers to change sexist restrictions on their participation in the Church's life.

Womanist theology is roughly two decades old; its long-term impact on the Black Church remains uncertain. Yet because many of the scholars involved in this area of study are also members of the Black Church—Cheryl Townsend Gilkes is a Baptist minister, theologian Cheryl Kirk-Duggan is a CME minister, Jacquelyn Grant is an AME minister—it is possible that their position as "insiders" may help them connect with women in the pews as well as men who are sympathetic to the issue. On the other hand, however, C. Eric Lincoln and Lawrence Mamiya demonstrate in their sociological study that the impact of black theology on the Church has been minimal outside of seminary-trained ministers, and even these ministers raise questions concerning the usefulness of academic, theological arguments within the practical context of church work.[32] Womanist theologians may confront the same problem with respect to their work. The upside is that over the course of its long history the Church has shown itself capable of change. And on this score, persistence may prove beneficial.

7

Future Considerations

Technology and Megachurches

Over the past several decades the world has become a smaller place. Information has become instantaneously available because of technological advances. Although new technology is initially expensive and beyond the reach of many Americans, companies have made an effort to produce equipment at a lower price in order to capture more of the consumer market. Virtually every home in the United States contains a television. Various "calling plans" put cell phones within the reach of most consumers. Efforts are being made to duplicate these successes with respect to home computers and access to the Internet. Technology's potential for enhancing the effectiveness with which ministry is carried out is not lost on religious individuals and communities concerned with expansive ministries. For example, the Institute of Church Administration and Management at the Interdenominational Theological Center in Atlanta, a major training ground for black ministers, offers courses on the Black Church and technology. In the words of Robert Franklin, the seminary's president, there is a need for a new type of ministry composed of leaders who are "technologically literate visionaries who experiment with new ways of using emerging technology to minister to the hunger for spiritual nourishment."[1]

Even the internal workings of the Black Church are being addressed through new technology. For example, during the AME Church's recent General Conference, voting took place not through the traditional ballet box but by computer.[2] Other large churches are known to use slide presentation software in order to provide visual aids during church activities. Still others make computer terminals available to allow congregants to download sermons and other information. And to address a general ignorance with respect to computers as a way of maximizing technology, churches, like God's Tabernacle AME Church, offer computer training classes.[3] Furthermore, many churches, thinking beyond the Sunday service, are encouraging members to participate in Internet conversations and other interactive opportunities. Evidence of this is the presence of websites devoted to all of the seven denominations except the National Baptist Convention of America, and numerous others launched by local congregations. Church websites often provide electronic bulletins for the denomination. Well-maintained sites provide working links and other up-to-date and useful information.

The Internet has made it possible to reach thousands, potentially millions, with the Church's message. In this way the Black Church can quickly and with fiscal effectiveness present its message to large groups in ways that individual services cannot match. Churches interested in tapping into this technology can make use of online networks, such as Christianity.com, which provide individuals and churches (of all denominations) with more services than are currently available through any one Internet site. That is to say, "Christianity.com . . . will equip individuals, churches, and organizations with a sophisticated network of services, and tools that give users a wide spectrum of online sources." Available services include assistance with construction of websites, web-based e-mail, eMarketing and eFunding.[4] A more focused Internet resource is BlackandChristian.com. With Jacqueline Trussell as its president, the site was launched on February 26, 2000, as a way of spreading information concerning the history and activities of black churches and the black Christian community in general. Trussell puts it this way: "As a former religious journalist, I know that there are many activities, events, and programs that take place with the Black Church that never get covered in the mainstream press. BlackandChristian.com is the voice for the African American Christian community and a means for sharing information and inspiration online."[5] In addition, the website also warehouses resources of particular interest to black Christians, thereby making the World Wide Web more manageable for a black church audience. Although the first year, according to Trussell, revolved around "designing the site, establishing content areas and features and building an audience and relationships," the site had received seventeen thousand hits. In order to increase this number, Trussell plans to publicize the site through church visits.[6] Plans are also underway to add new links as well as features such as instant messaging. Trussell sees potential but is not extremely optimistic that congregations will make great strides with respect to Internet use. In her words: "There are still too many churches and pastors that are not interested or do not have an understanding themselves [of the Internet]. . . . Some don't trust technology. . . . In many cases the problem is not with the pastor but with untrained staff or the lack of staff to use a computer and explore its usefulness."[7] Nonetheless, it seems that larger churches, often referred to as megachurches, are making tremendous strides with respect to enhanced ministry through technology.

The Megachurches

As of 1991, an estimated forty-five churches in the United States had five thousand or more worshipers on a given Sunday. Now there are more than four hundred such churches, thirty-five of which are black churches.[8] The style of these black megachurches (congregations with over three thousand members) is not easily defined. Some are charismatic; others evangelical; some traditional members of major black denominations; others nondenominational. Many of these churches began to develop in part spurred by the movement of black "baby boomers" into suburban areas. However, this does not explain the growth of all megachurches, and it certainly does not account for the success over the past several decades of figures like Fred Price, whose church remains located in urban Los Angeles. Beginning in 1969 with nine members, Price's Crenshaw Christian Center has grown to a congregation of eighteen thousand and a television viewership of 33 million (1999). The congregation became far too big for its sanctuary. To accommodate the growth, the $9 million FaithDome was built on thirty-two acres. "The FaithDome is a geodesic facility made of high-strength aluminum instead of the more conventional steel. The massive building is designed theater-style with sky-blue seats and matching carpeting, and there are no pillars or columns. Overhead lights help obscure the potential distraction of the aluminum, cross-hatched ceiling."[9]

At times during his long career Price was at odds with black worship tradition and tended toward the conservative theology of white evangelicals, but the church's contemporary work marks a new direction. For example, unlike some televangelists and megachurch pastors, Price has recently spoken out against racism within the country, even arguing that "religion has been the most flagrant perpetrator of racism in the world. In particular the Christian Church in America has been the leader of racism in the world and particularly in America."[10] Current programming by the church such as the "Race, Religion, and Racism" series addresses this issue. The church also has developed a variety of ministries including a school, day-care center, and alcohol and drug-abuse programs in order to address pressing socioeconomic issues.

During the same time that Price was beginning his ministry, Johnnie Colemon was starting her Christ Universal Temple in Chicago. Beginning with thirty-five members, by 1990 it claimed a membership of ten thousand and a church building valued at over $10 million.

A much more recent development, but no less influential, is the Potter's House Ministries of Dallas, pastored by the widely known T. D. Jakes. Moving from smaller ministries to Temple of Faith Ministries in South Carolina, Jakes eventually moved to Dallas in 1996 and started the Potter's House Ministries, which currently claims twenty-six thousand members. In addition to typical church-based ministries, Jakes makes use of technology through a weekly television show ("Get Ready with T. D. Jakes") aired on Black Entertainment Television. He is also known for the fourteen books he has written, many of them Christian best-sellers, as well as national conferences with attendance as high as fifty thousand.

Although many of the megachurches are nondenominational, several of them are located within the major black denominations discussed in this book. The Bethel AME Church in Baltimore is a prime example. This church of over 10,000 members is pastored by Frank Madison Reid and provides a full range of services. The West Angeles Church of God in Christ (Los Angeles) mentioned elsewhere in this text claims some 15,000 members. Among the largest, however, is the Full Gospel African Methodist Episcopal Zion Church in Maryland, which has 21,000 members on the church roll. Furthermore, over the course of the past three decades many of the local churches within the major denominations have developed memberships of well over 3,000 and as a result now can be considered megachurches. They include Hartford Memorial Baptist Church of Detroit (10,000 members), Ebenezer AME Church of Maryland (10,000 members), and Allen AME Church (over 9,000). Like the others, these churches must wrestle with what it means to be relevant to a large population that represents the full socioeconomic and political spectrum and often has competing interests.

Impact of the Megachurch Phenomenon

These large churches by nature are somewhat impersonal and, for some, this counters the purpose of religious fellowship and church membership.

There is no doubt that these churches have the financial resources and personnel necessary to do good work with respect to socioeconomic and political issues. And many have programs going on for so many hours of the day that they are referred to as "seven-day-a-week" churches. But the possibility of losing the personal touch looms large. "Some churches are growing and prospering based on a formula that emphasizes financial stewardship, Bible literacy and membership training—often mandatory. All serve to bond individuals tightly to their church, though some say this growth strategy threatens a more personal Christian fellowship."[11] Yet, ministers such as Frank Reid argue that "the central tenet that all of the megachurches have is meeting the needs of God's people."[12] This is easier said than done. In smaller churches members have more contact with the pastor and are able to secure more quality time with respect to their spiritual questions and needs. But within megachurches it would be impossible for the senior minister actually to have real contact with the members. How does one person deal directly with thousands of people? In order to service members, megachurches must creatively develop ministerial staffs that are able to function independent of the pastor while maintaining the pastor's vision for the church. If not, this complaint from a disgruntled parishioner will be spoken in an increasing number of churches: "It just felt like spiritual enrichment needed to be more personal. I felt like I didn't matter."[13]

In the long run, it is likely that a needs-based approach to ministry will dominate in churches with large numbers as well as those attempting to gain large numbers. The basic theological parameters will soften to accommodate this form of ministry. For example, it is likely that churches will interpret the message of the New Testament so that Jesus speaks favorably to the acquisition of goods. Marketing and public relations companies will help churches develop the language and appeal necessary to increase their audience. In this respect the organizational language of these large black churches will shift its center from doctrine to corporate jargon. The attitude of those seeking religious community will also change, with a closer resemblance to what in the past had been reserved for consumer purchases. It also remains to be seen if the megachurch phenomenon will enhance black Christians' abilities to influence broad political and economic issues that affect more than a small geographic area. Indeed, the gospel of prosperity that is preached in many of the more sizable churches may serve to hamper this national thrust. "There is a tendency right now among Black Church men to be at ease in Zion, to kind of feel that everything is okay in the area of race and social justice, and to concentrate primarily on building our buildings and preaching success to our people."[14] This prosperity thrust is much softer on controversial issues and tends to amplify individual growth over national consciousness. One gets a hint of this in the mission statement for T. D. Jakes's Potter's House Ministries: "T. D. Jakes Ministries endeavors to contribute to the spiritual, relational and entrepreneurial advancement of the Christian community by providing biblical enrichment, spiritual guidance, motivational resources and economic empowerment. Bishop Jakes hopes that his ministry will enable Christians to overcome personal obstacles and limitations and adopt a zeal for advancement."[15]

There are, of course, numerous exceptions to this prosperity emphasis—churches mentioned in the previous several chapters attest to this—but the number of megachurches preaching this material gospel remains high, and the message maintains its appeal with those who have achieved a level of success because it allows spiritual renewal without the burden or guilt often associated with "making it." Many who seek material advancement also appreciate the message because it does not suggest that a Christlike existence entails a vow of poverty. Rather, these churches argue that God desires all Christians to have material comfort and individual salvation, and "the problem with that is individual salvation becomes as selfish as the greed motive in America."[16] Black Churches, like all churches, need to ask this question as they move into the twenty-first century: Is religion a commodity, a product?

This question and the larger debate over the so-called gospel of prosperity are not simply an attack on an assumed crude materialism. T. D.

Jakes and others are not really advocating a consumerism defined by prosperity at all cost. That is to say, against popular depictions, these megachurches are not advocating acquisition or material success as an end in and of itself. Rather, they preach the merits of proper relationship with God and with humanity; in turn, these proper relationships make possible various blessing from God. It is, to some extent, a version of Calvinism's perspective on material success as the byproduct of healthy spirituality. Yet there is a certain hazard to face, one other forms of Calvinism have faced. It is more than likely that this gospel of prosperity in a world of economic injustice easily devolves and becomes a religious cover for materiality, reading spiritual growth and material acquisition as synonymous.

Finally, as the twenty-first century begins, even black churches that have no interest in the megachurch phenomenon are likely to find themselves forced to respond. It is possible that these megachurches, particularly the nondenominational ones, will challenge the vitality of more traditionally aligned denominational churches because of their doctrinal and structural flexibility. Whether an active participant or not, black churches in the twenty-first century will have no choice but to think about their ministries and audience in terms of the megachurch phenomenon and its interpretation of the gospel.

Chronology

What follows are some of the important dates in the development of the Black Church, with respect to its constituency, institutional form, theology, and activities.

1619	Enslaved Africans arrive in Virginia
1641	Earliest recorded account of an African Church member (Massachusetts)
1702	Society for the Propagation of the Gospel in Foreign Parts attempts to convert slaves
1773	First black church (Baptist) formed—Silver Bluff Church
1780-1830	Second Great Awakening
1787	Free African Society formed in Philadelphia
1796	Black Methodists form a church in New York
1801	The 1796 church incorporated as the African Methodist Episcopal Church of New York
1816	AME Church denomination formed
1821	1796 church and others form a new Methodist conference
1824	The African Methodist Episcopal Church in America formed from the 1821 conference
1829	*David Walker's Appeal* published
1831	Maria Stewart becomes the first woman to lecture in public on religio-political issues
1834	Black Baptist associations begin to form
1848	*Zion* added to the name of the African Methodist Episcopal Church in America
1863	Emancipation Proclamation issued and Great Migration begins

1864	AME and AMEZ churches consider merger
1866	First state-wide Baptist convention forms
1870	Colored Methodist Episcopal Church formed
1871	Fisk Jubilee Singers begins popularizing spirituals
1873	Hampton Institute Singers begin revising spirituals
1894	Julia A. Foote ordained in the AME Zion Church
1895	National Baptist Convention, U.S.A., Inc., formed
1895	National Federation of Afro-American Women founded
1896	National Association of Colored Women formed
1896	Charles Mason forms the Church of God
1897	Mason's Church of God renamed Church of God in Christ
1897	First ordination of a female elder, Mary Small, in the AMEZ Church
1900	National Baptist Convention, U.S.A., Inc., forms its Woman's Convention
1903	W. E. B. Du Bois's *Souls of Black Folk* published
1906	Asuza Street Pentecostal revival begins
1915	National Baptist Convention of America formed
1932	Golden age of gospel music begins when Thomas Dorsey writes "Take My Hand, Precious Lord"
1948	CME Church ordains women local ministers
1948	AME Church ordains Rebecca M. Glover
1954	Colored Methodist Episcopal church becomes Christian Methodist Episcopal church (CME)
1955	Civil rights movement begins
1957	Interdenominational Theological Center founded
1957	Southern Christian Leadership Conference formed
1961	Progressive National Baptist Convention formed
1963	Martin L. King, Jr., issues the "Letter from a Birmingham Jail"
1966	CME Church ordains Virgie Amanda Jackson Ghant

1966	Full clergy rights for women in CME Church
1966	National Committee of Black Churchmen (NCBC) formed
1967	King develops the Poor People's Campaign
1967	First Black Power conference held
1968	Civil rights movement under King ends with his assassination
1969	The "Black Manifesto" presented by James Forman at the Detroit meeting of the National Black Economic Development Conference
1969	Black liberation theology forms as academic discipline
1970	Society for the Study of Black Religion founded
1970s-1980s	Decline in church membership in some denominations
1970s-1990s	Increased media attention on celebrities becoming ministers
1971	Operation PUSH is initiated.
1977	First Black Theology Project meeting held
1978	Partners in Ecumenism (PIE) formed
1978	Congress of National Black Churches formed
1978	Project SPIRIT developed to help five of the seven major denominations address educational issues in black communities
1979	First article in womanist theology published
1980s-1990s	Church burnings gain media headlines
1982	A group of black churchwomen lead a protest in Warren County, North Carolina, to prevent the dumping of toxic waste in its community
1983	AME Bishop Philip Cousins becomes the first National Council of Churches of Christ president from a black denomination
1983	Eco-Justice Working Group formed
1984	Rev. Jesse Jackson runs for president of the United States
1985	First text in womanist ethics published
1987	First text using term *womanist theology* published
1987	"Report on Race and Toxic Wastes in the United States" issued by the United Church of Christ Commission of Racial Justice, with participation from a few of the major black denominations

1988	National Missionary Baptist Convention of America splits from the National Baptist Convention of America
1988	Rev. Jesse Jackson runs for president of the United States
1989	First Black Church Week of Prayer for the Healing of AIDS takes place
1989	National Baptist Convention, U.S.A., Inc., completes construction of the first "World Center" built by a black denomination
1990s	General movement of the black middle class back into black churches
1990s	Growth in number of megachurches, many marked by a "gospel of prosperity"
1991	First National People of Color Environmental Leadership Summit
1991	AME Bishop Vinton R. Anderson named first black president of the World Council of Churches
1992-1996	Interfaith Health Program (Carter Center) in operation
1993	National Council of Churches in cooperation with several of the black denominations holds the National Black Church Environmental and Economic Justice Summit
1998	Religious Coalition for Reproductive Choice sponsors the National Black Religious Summit II
1999	Henry J. Lyons convicted of racketeering and grand theft and resigns presidency of the National Baptist Convention, U.S.A., Inc.
2000	Vashti Murphy McKenzie elected first woman bishop in the AME Church

Notes

Every effort has been made to ensure that the URLs in the following notes are accurate and up to date. However, with the rapid changes that occur in the World Wide Web, it is inevitable that some pages or other resources will have been discontinued or moved, and some content modified or reorganized. The publisher recommends that readers who cannot find the sources or information they seek with the URLs below use one of the numerous search engines available on the Internet.

Introduction

1. Clarence Taylor, *The Black Churches of Brooklyn* (New York: Columbia University Press, 1994), 7.

2. See, for example, Carter Godwin Woodson, *The History of the Negro Church*, 2d ed. (Washington, D.C.: The Associated Publishers, 1945); Benjamin E. Mays, *The Negro's Church* (New York, Arno Press, 1969); C. Eric Lincoln, *The Black Church since Frazier* (with E. Franklin Frazier's *The Negro Church in America*) (New York: Schocken Books, 1974).

3. <http://www.barna.org/cgi-bin/MainArchives.asp>

4. For some of these other traditions, see Anthony B. Pinn, *Varieties of African American Religious Experience* (Minneapolis: Fortress Press, 1998); a second volume, *Varieties of African American Religious Experience II,* should be completed by 2004.

5. C. Eric Lincoln and Lawrence Mamiya, *The Black Church in the African American Experience* (Durham, N.C.: Duke University Press, 1990), 144.

6. Gayraud S. Wilmore, *Black Religion and Black Radicalism: An Interpretation of the Religious History of Afro-American People,* 2d ed. (Maryknoll, N.Y.: Orbis Books, 1983), x.

7. Andrew Billingsley, *Mighty Like a River: The Black Church and Social Reform* (New York: Oxford University Press, 1999), 198-206.

8. Charles Long, *Significations: Signs, Symbols, and Images in the Interpretation of Religion* (Philadelphia: Fortress Press, 1986; Aurora, Colo.: Davies Group, 1999), 9.

9. Ibid., 7.

10. For additional information on the history of the Black Church prior to 1970, see Anthony B. Pinn and Anne H. Pinn, *The Fortress Introduction to Black Church History* (Minneapolis: Fortress Press, 2001).

Part I
Historical and Theological Background

1 Themes in Black Church History, 1864 to 1970

1. William E. Montgomery, *Under Their Own Vine and Fig Tree: The African-American Church in the South, 1865-1900* (Baton Rouge, La.: Louisiana State University Press, 1993), 66.

2. In ibid.

3. Ibid., 89.

4. C. Eric Lincoln and Lawrence Mamiya, *The Black Church in the African American Experience* (Durham, N.C.: Duke University Press, 1990), 45.

5. Levi Coppin, "The Negro's Part in the Redemption of Africa," *AME Church Review* 19 (October 1902), in *The Social Protest Thought of the African Methodist Episcopal Church, 1862-1939*, ed. Stephen Angell and Anthony Pinn (Knoxville, Tenn.: The University of Tennessee Press, 2000), 218.

6. Lincoln and Mamiya, *The Black Church in the African American Experience*, 84.

7. Alexander Crummell, "The Regeneration of Africa," in *Afro-American Religious History: A Documentary Witness*, ed. Milton C. Sernett (Durham, N.C.: Duke University Press, 1985), 254.

8. Lawrence S. Little, *Disciples of Liberty: The African Methodist Episcopal Church in the Age of Imperialism, 1884-1916* (Knoxville, Tenn.: The University of Tennessee Press, 2000), 70.

9. Gayraud Wilmore, *Black Religion and Black Radicalism: An Interpretation of the Religious History of Afro-American People*, 2d ed. (Maryknoll, N.Y.: Orbis Books, 1983), 143. Furthermore, if one takes into consideration the movement out of the South that continued through the end of the 1960s, more than 7 million black Americans migrated to the North during that period.

10. John Hope Franklin, *From Slavery to Freedom: A History of Negro Americans*, 5th ed. (New York: Alfred A. Knopf, 1980), 281.

11. Quoted in Milton C. Sernett, *Bound for the Promised Land: African American Religion and the Great Migration* (Durham, N.C.: Duke University Press, 1997), 76.

12. Ibid., 77.

13. Ibid., 88.

14. Theodore Kornweibel, Jr., "City and Suburb since 1940," in *In Search of the Promised Land: Essays in Black Urban History*, ed. T. Kornweibel (Port Washington, N.Y.: Kennikat Press, 1981), 182.

15. Manning Marable, *How Capitalism Underdeveloped Black America* (Boston: South End Press, 1983), Introduction.

16. Reverdy C. Ransom, "The Institutional Church," *Christian Recorder* (March 7, 1901), reprinted in *Making the Gospel Plain: The Writings of Bishop Reverdy C. Ransom*, ed. Anthony B. Pinn (Harrisburg, Pa.: Trinity Press International, 1999), 198.

17. African Methodist Episcopal Church, "The Mission and Purpose of the Church," *The Doctrine and Discipline of the African Methodist Episcopal Church, 1996-2000* (Nashville, Tenn.: AMEC Sunday School Union, 1996), 12.

18. Phyl Garland, "I Remember Adam: TV Documentary Revives Interest in Rep. Adam Clayton Powell, Jr.," *Ebony Magazine* (March 1990), 56, 58.

19. Anne Standley, "The Role of Black Women in the Civil Rights Movement," in *Women in the Civil Rights Movement: Trailblazers and Torchbearers, 1941-1965,* ed. Vicki L. Crawford et al. (Brooklyn, N.Y.: Carlson Publishing, Inc., 1990), 188.

20. Martin Luther King, Jr., *The Autobiography of Martin Luther King, Jr.,* ed. Clayborne Carson (New York: Warner Books, 1998), 65.

21. Mary Fair Burks, "Traiblazers: Women in the Montgomery Bus Boycott," in Crawford et al., *Women in the Civil Rights Movement,* 80.

22. I have in mind the de-radicalization of black churches that marks the period between the Great Migration to the civil rights movement, during which black churches were marked by a decidedly otherworldly orientation. For an insightful treatment of this, see Wilmore, *Black Religion and Black Radicalism.* A discussion of these two movements is beyond the scope of this essay, but for readers interested in this information, the following provide important insights: Stokely Carmichael and Charles V. Hamilton, *Black Power: The Politics of Liberation in America* (New York: Vintage Books, 1967); Floyd B. Barbour, comp., *The Black Power Revolt: A Collection of Essays* (Boston: P. Sargent, 1968); Clayborne Carson, *In Struggle: SNCC and the Black Awakening of the 1960s* (Cambridge, Mass.: Harvard University Press, 1981); Martin L. King, *Where Do We Go from Here: Chaos or Community?* (New York: Harper & Row, 1967); Malcolm X, *The Last Speeches,* ed. Steve Clark (New York: Pathfinder Press, 1992); Taylor Branch, *Parting the Waters: America in the King Years, 1954-63* (New York: Simon & Schuster, 1988); Taylor Branch, *Pillar of Fire: America in the King Years, 1963-65* (New York: Simon & Schuster, 1998). In terms of documentary treatments, readers should be aware of "Eyes on the Prize: America at the Racial Crossroads" (Alexandria, Va.: PBS Video, 1986, 1990).

23. James H. Cone, *For My People: Black Theology and the Black Church, Where Have We Been and Where Are We Going?* (Maryknoll, N.Y.: Orbis Books, 1984), 199.

2 Themes in Black Church History, 1970 to the Present

1. Benjamin E. Mays, quoted in Mark L. Chapman, *Christianity on Trial: African-American Religious Thought before and after Black Power* (Maryknoll, N.Y.: Orbis Books, 1996), 25.

2. Peter Paris, *The Social Teaching of the Black Churches* (Philadelphia: Fortress Press, 1985), 112.

3. Ella Baker, quoted in Carol Mueller, "Ella Baker and the Origins of 'Participatory Democracy,'" in *Women in the Civil Rights Movement: Trailblazers and Torchbearers, 1941-1965,* ed. Vicki L. Crawford, et al. (Brooklyn, N.Y.: Carlson Publishing, Inc., 1990), 60.

4. Dennis W. Wiley, "Black Theology, the Black Church, and the African-American Community," in *Black Theology: A Documentary History, Volume 2: 1980-1992,* ed. James H. Cone and Gayraud S. Wilmore (Maryknoll, N.Y.: Orbis Books, 1993), 135.

5. C. Eric Lincoln and Lawrence Mamiya, *The Black Church in the African American Experience* (Durham, N.C.: Duke University Press, 1990), 136.

6. Charles Adams, "Burden of Black Religion," Hartford Memorial Baptist Church, Detroit, Michigan (April 12, 1992), cassette tape. Quoted in Fredrick C. Harris, *Something Within: Religion in African-American Political Activism* (New York: Oxford University Press, 1999), 5.

7. Adolph Reed, quoted in Harris, *Something Within*, 6.

8. Beverly Hall Lawrence, *Reviving the Spirit: A Generation of African Americans Goes Home to Church* (New York: Grove Press, 1996), 15-16.

9. Stephen L. Carter, *The Culture of Disbelief* (New York: Basic Books, 1993), 6-7.

10. Farai Chicara, "Money, Power, Respect?" *Emerge Magazine* (October 1998), 34.

11. David George, "Changing Face of the Black Church in U.S." (December 18, 1995): <http://www.cnn.com/EVENT/world_of_faith/9512/black_church/>

12. Rev. Jamal Harrison Bryant, quoted in Lottie L. Joiner, "Youth Quest," *Emerge Magazine* (June 1997), 35.

13. Lincoln and Mamiya, *The Black Church in the African American Experience*, 316.

14. Arrested Development, "Fishin' 4 Religion," on *Three Years, 5 Months, and 2 Days in the Life of . . .* (New York: Chrysalis Records, 1992).

15. James H. Cone, *A Black Theology of Liberation*, 2d ed. (Maryknoll, N.Y.: Orbis Books, 1986), 65.

16. James H. Cone, *Black Theology and Black Power*, 20th anniv. ed. (New York: Harper & Row, 1989), 143.

17. Martin Luther King, Jr., *The Autobiography of Martin Luther King, Jr.*, ed. Clayborne Carson (New York: Warner Books, 1998), 328, 331.

18. Cone, *Black Theology and Black Power*, 140.

19. Cone, *A Black Theology of Liberation*, 56.

20. James H. Cone, *For My People: Black Theology and the Black Church, Where Have We Been and Where Are We Going?* (Maryknoll, N.Y.: Orbis Books, 1984), 199.

21. James H. Harris, "Black Church and Black Theology: Theory and Practice," in Cone and Wilmore, *Black Theology*, 85.

22. Cone, *For My People*, 114.

23. Ibid., 114-15.

24. Renée Leslie Hill, "Disrupted/Disruptive Movements: Black Theology and Black Power 1969/1999," in *Black Faith and Public Talk: Critical Essays on James H. Cone's Black Theology and Black Power*, ed. Dwight N. Hopkins (Maryknoll, N.Y.: Orbis Books, 1999), 145.

25. J. Alfred Smith, Sr., "Black Theology and the Parish Ministry," in Hopkins, *Black Faith and Public Talk*, 91-92.

26. Sonsyrea Tate, *Little X: Growing Up in the Nation of Islam* (San Francisco: HarperSanFrancisco, 1997), 3.

27. Jane Smith, *Islam in America* (New York: Columbia University Press, 1999), 150.

28. Lincoln and Mamiya, *The Black Church in the African American Experience*, 382.

29. Martha Sawyer Allen, "A Fast-Growing Church Is on the Move," *Star Tribune* (September 26, 1993).

30. Clarissa Wells, quoted in ibid.

31. Most churches have a paid minister and a rather small staff, most of whom are volunteers and a few of whom receive only small compensation for their services. These churches typically have a musician and a secretary. There may also be ministerial staff (paid or not) who assist with the spiritual concerns of the church. The average black minister, who is more than fifty years old, has a rather modest income and range of benefits.

32. Cornel West, "The Paradox of the African American Rebellion," in *Keeping Faith: Philosophy and Race in America* (New York: Routledge, 1993), 283.

33. Alphonos Pinkney, *The Myth of Black Progress* (New York: Cambridge University Press, 1984), 106.

34. Hall Lawrence, *Reviving the Spirit*, 16.

35. In some cases churches relocated to suburban neighborhoods as a way of keeping more financially sound members who found the commute to an inner-city church problematic. For other churches, the move to the suburbs was necessitated by the unavailability of cheap land to expand inner-city churches growing as a result of new black professional members (Fred A. Lucas's presentation during the Harvard Divinity School Conference entitled "A New Urban Agenda: The Black Church's Economic Responsibility," 1994 [video #2 "Models of Church and Community Development"]).

36. Richard N. Ostling, "Strains on the Heart: U.S. Black Churches Battle Apathy and Threats to Their Relevance But Also Revel in Renewal," *Time Magazine* (November 19, 1990), 90.

37. Hall Lawrence, *Reviving the Spirit*, 66-67.

38. Sidney Verba, cited in Harris, *Something Within*, 97.

39. Helen Oliver, "Clergy Sexual Misconduct: A Lay Perspective," *AME Church Review* (October-December 1998), 32.

40. Cornel West, "The Making of an American Radical Democrat of African Descent," in *The Cornel West Reader*, ed. Cornel West (New York: Basic Civitas Books, 1999), 17.

41. Quoted in Harris, *Something Within*, 104.

42. Ibid., 111.

43. Tatsha Roberts, "Many Blacks Find Faith," and Susan Hogan Albach, "Black Churches Leaving Inner City," *Star Tribune* (Minneapolis-St. Paul) (December 21, 1997).

44. Barbara Eklof, quoted in J. Deotis Roberts, *Africentric Christianity: A Theological Appraisal for Ministry* (Valley Forge, Pa.: Judson Press, 2000).

45. Ibid.

46. Herert H. Toler, Jr., "Fisher of Men: A Baltimore Minister Promotes Black Christian Manhood," *AME Church Review* (April-June 1995), 12.

47. Ibid., 16.

48. The numbers for the individual denominations are as follows:

> AME Church—3,500,000
> AMEZ Church—1,200,000
> CME Church—719,000
> COGIC—5,500,000
> National Baptist Convention, U.S.A., Inc.—8,200,000
> National Baptist Convention of America—3,500,000
> Progressive National Baptist Convention—2,500,000

49. See "The Human Face of Hate Crimes," at <http://www.civilrights.org/publications/cause_for_concern/p8.html>

50. Ron Nixon and Dennis Bernstein, "Mississippi Burnings: Who's Torching Black Churches, and Why Hasn't the Massive Investigation Cleared the Smoke?" *Vibe Magazine* (October 1996), 95-96. Of course, numbers vary depending on the source. However, it is clear that the majority of these acts have been against black and predominantly black churches.

51. "The Human Face of Hate Crimes."

52. Nixon and Bernstein, "Mississippi Burnings," 97.

53. Pamela Berry, quoted in ibid., 98.

3 Beliefs and Worship in the Black Church

1. Norman W. Brown, "What the Negro Thinks of God," in *Social Protest Thought in the African Methodist Episcopal Church, 1862-1939*, ed. Stephen Angell and Anthony Pinn (Knoxville, Tenn.: University of Tennessee Press, 2000), 137.

2. James H. Cone, *A Black Theology of Liberation* (Maryknoll, N.Y.: Orbis Books, 1986), 63.

3. <http://www.cogic.org/believe.htm>

4. Quoted in Beverly Hall Lawrence, *Reviving the Spirit: A Generation of African Americans Goes Home to Church* (New York: Grove Press, 1996), 52.

5. <http://religiousmovements.lib.virginia.edu/nrms/nbc_usa.html>

6. Interview with Rev. Anne H. Pinn (March 3, 2001).

7. <http://www.cogic.org/doctrine.htm>

8. C. Eric Lincoln and Lawrence Mamiya, *The Black Church in the African American Experience* (Durham, N.C.: Duke University Press, 1990), 386.

9. Peter Paris, *The Social Teaching of the Black Churches* (Philadelphia: Fortress Press, 1985), 60.

10. George D. McKinney, *I Will Build My Church* (St. Louis: Open Door Ministries, 1985), 19.

11. Kelly Miller Smith Institute, "What Does It Mean to Be Black and Christian?," in *Black Theology: A Documentary History, Volume 2: 1980-1992*, ed. James H. Cone and Gayraud S. Wilmore (Maryknoll, N.Y.: Orbis Books, 1993), 168.

12. Albert Raboteau, *Slave Religion: The "Invisible Institution" in the Antebellum South* (New York: Oxford University Press, 1978), 241.

13. Martin L. King, Jr., "Letter from Birmingham Jail," in *The Autobiography of Martin Luther King, Jr.*, ed. Clayborne Carson (New York: Warner Books, 1998), 189.

14. McKinney, *I Will Build My Church*, 14-15.

15. Elisabeth Schüssler Fiorenza, quoted in James Evans, *We Have Been Believers: An African-American Systematic Theology* (Minneapolis: Fortress Press, 1992), 48.

16. Katie Cannon, "Womanist Interpretation and Preaching in the Black Church," in Katie Cannon, *Katie's Canon: Womanism and the Soul of the Black Community* (New York: Continuum, 1995), 121.

17. H. A. Chambers, ed., *The Treasury of Negro Spirituals* (New York: Emerson Books, 1963), 48.

18. John Lovell, Jr., *Black Song: The Forge and the Flame; The Story of How the Afro American Spiritual Was Hammered Out* (New York: MacMillan, 1972), 258-62.

19. Ibid., 23.

20. Walter Pitts discusses this and provides an interesting discussion of European musical developments relevant to the formation of revival music (see *Old Ship of Zion: The Afro-Baptist Ritual in the African Diaspora* [New York: Oxford University Press, 1993]).

21. Spirituals do not represent the only form of musical expression developed by enslaved Africans. Scholars of black American music such as Dena Epstein point to the work songs associated with agricultural work, domestic work, boat-related employment, and other forms of employment. These songs served to pass the long workday and to regulate the rhythm of work. Whites usually encouraged the performance of these songs because they assumed the joy of singing would increase productivity and reduce troublesome conversation. Those working in cities made use of rhythmic "street cries" to bring attention to their services and goods. In addition, and more recognizable from Hollywood depictions of the 1800s, are the dances and songs associated with holidays and leisure time. It was with this form of song that instruments—those permitted—were utilized.

22. Ira Berlin, Marc Favreau, and Steven F. Miller, eds., *Remembering Slavery: African Americans Talk about Their Personal Experiences of Slavery and Emancipation* (New York: The New Press, 1998), 195-96.

23. Raboteau, *Slave Religion*, 245-46.

24. This, of course, was not always the case. In many blues tunes the sense of religion and reverence for God is in keeping with what would have been preached in most churches. For a more detailed and more highly nuanced discussion on this subject and related concerns, see Jon Michael Spencer, *Blues and Evil* (Knoxville, Tenn.: The University of Tennessee Press, 1993). This book also provides a useful discussion of the typical misunderstandings presented in blues scholarship.

25. Mahalia Jackson, "Singing of Good Tidings and Freedom," in *Afro-American Religious History: A Documentary Witness*, ed. Milton C. Sernett (Durham, N.C.: Duke University Press, 1985), 451-52.

26. For a concise discussion of music during this period, see Cornel West, "On Afro-American Music: From Bebop to Rap," in West, *The Cornel West Reader*. For a more detailed discussion, see Nelson George, *The Death of Rhythm and Blues* (New York: Pantheon, 1988).

27. Melva Wilson Costen, *African American Christian Worship* (Nashville, Tenn.: Abingdon Press, 1993), 103-4.

28. It is interesting to note, however, that gospel singer Marion Williams was the first to be honored by the Kennedy Center in Washington, D.C., and is credited with influencing secular performers such as Little Richard (see "Gospel Divas," *Ebony Magazine* [April 1994], 78).

29. Albertina Walker, quoted in ibid.

30. Rev. Milton Brunson, quoted in Karima A. Haynes, "The Gospel Controversy: Are the New Songs Too Jazzy and Too Worldly?" *Ebony Magazine* (March 1992), 78.

31. Alan Light, "Say Amen, Somebody!" *Vibe Magazine* (October 1997), 92.

32. Over the past decade, hip hop and gospel have come together in other ways, most noticeably with the development of gospel rap by groups such as Gospel Gangstas and artist Nuwine. Nuwine argues that his music is not necessarily "religious" in a strict sense. Rather, it is his attempt to discuss the events of his life that eventually led him to the Church. During various interviews, Nuwine, who records on boxer Evander Holyfield's label, has talked about his early childhood. As a preteen he dropped out of school and became involved in gang activity. In 1990 this activity resulted in gunfire. This experience did not stop the activities that eventually took him before a judge. But at that point, while awaiting his court appearance, he had a conversion experience. After this conversion experience, Nuwine began using his rap abilities to spread the story of his transformed life. Beginning with CDs sold from his trunk, he produced music that moved beyond the mere nihilism present in some rap to a modest optimism based on the Christian faith. Nuwine argues that his music may be a little "hard," but that is appropriate because it speaks to people who are in need.

33. "Hottest Gospel Artists," *Ebony Magazine* (August 1998), 74.

34. Kirk Franklin, quoted in Lisa C. Jones, "Kirk Franklin: New Gospel Sensation," *Ebony Magazine* (October 1995), 66; also see Light, "Say Amen, Somebody!," 91.

35. Jackson, "Singing of Good Tidings and Freedom," 453-54.

36. See Henry H. Mitchell, *Black Preaching: The Recovery of a Powerful Art*, reprint ed. (Nashville, Tenn.: Abingdon Press, 1990); William H. Pipes, *Say Amen, Brother!: Old Negro Preaching: A Study in American Frustration* (Detroit, Mich.: Wayne State University Press, 1992).

37. Berlin, Favreau, and Miller, *Remembering Slavery*, 191.

38. Raboteau, *Slave Religion*, 235-36.

39. As late as the early 1970s most ministers lacked any formal training, and many local churches maintained an anti-intellectual attitude that assumed formal training reduced one's "openness" to direction from God; that is, human wisdom negated godly influence. According to C. Eric Lincoln and Lawrence Mamiya's 1990 study of black churches, most of the ministers in rural settings had little college training. The numbers were better for ministers in urban settings, with roughly 70 percent having some degree of college education. However, educational level within both groups has shown continual growth over the past six decades, with many denominations urging education beyond the undergraduate level.

40. John R. Bryant, "Our Father, the King," in *Preaching on Suffering and a God of Love,* ed. Henry J. Young (Philadelphia: Fortress Press, 1978).

41. Gardner C. Taylor, *Scarlet Thread: Nineteen Sermons* (Elgin, Ill.: Progressive Baptist Publishing House, 1981), Foreword.

42. Samuel D. Proctor, Gardner C. Taylor, with Gary V. Simpson, *We Have This Ministry: The Heart of the Pastor's Vocation* (Valley Forge, Pa.: Judson Press, 1996), 115.

43. Cheryl J. Sanders, "The Woman as Preacher," in *African American Religious Studies: An Interdisciplinary Anthology*, ed. Gayraud Wilmore (Durham, N.C.: Duke University Press, 1989), 376.

44. Johnny Ray Youngblood, quoted in Samuel G. Freedman, *Upon This Rock: The Miracles of a Black Church* (New York: HarperCollins Publishers, 1993), 13.

45. Dr. Jeremiah A. Wright, Jr., "If Only He Knew . . . ," sermon preached at Trinity United Church of Christ, Chicago, October 26, 1986, 11 A.M. service.

46. Rev. C. L. Franklin, "The Eagle Stirreth Her Nest," sermon preached at New Bethel Baptist Church, Detroit.

47. Mitchell, *Black Preaching*, 98.

48. Henry H. Mitchell, "Toward a Theology of Black Preaching," in Wilmore, *African American Religious Studies*, 369.

49. "God Struck Me Dead," in *God Struck Me Dead: Religious Conversion Experiences and Autobiographies of Ex-slaves*, ed. Clifton H. Johnson (Boston: Pilgrim Press, 1969), 59.

50. Clifton H. Johnson, "Preface," in Johnson, *God Struck Me Dead*, v.

51. James Melvin Washington, ed., *Conversations with God: Two Centuries of Prayers by African Americans* (New York: Harper Publishers, 1994), xxiii.

52. "Henry Baker Interviewed, 1938, Alabama, by Thomas Campbell," in *Slave Testimony: Two Centuries of Letters, Speeches, Interviews, and Autobiographies*, ed. John W. Blassingame (Baton Rouge, La.: Louisiana State University Press, 1977), 673.

53. Washington, *Conversations with God*, xxx.

54. Andrew P. Watson, "Negro Primitive Religious Services," in Johnson, *God Struck Me Dead*, 3-4.

55. Frank Madison Reid, III, "A Prayer for Liberation That Leads to Liberating Love," in Washington, *Conversations with God*, 276.

Part II
Themes in Contemporary Praxis

4 The Black Church on Economic Issues

1. See Jacqueline Jones, *The Dispossessed: America's Underclass from the Civil War to the Present* (New York: Basic Books, 1992), chap. 9. A slightly altered version of this chapter will be published as "Of God, Money, and Earth: The Black Church on Economics and Environmental Racism," *The Journal of Religious Thought* 56/2, 57/1.

2. Donna L. Franklin, *Ensuring Inequality: The Structural Transformation of the African-American Family* (New York: Oxford University Press, 1997), 182.

3. Orlando Patterson, *The Ordeal of Integration* (Washington: Civitas/Counterpoint, 1997), 25.

4. Ibid.

5. Ibid.

6. <http://www.pnbc.org>

7. Religious News Service, "Black Baptist Groups to Detail Economic Partnership," *AME Church Review* (October-December 1995), 22.

8. <http://www.cogicmissions.org/goals2000.htm>

9. Hans A. Baer and Merrill Singer, *African-American Religion in the Twentieth Century: Varieties of Protest and Accommodation* (Nashville, Tenn.: University of Tennessee Press, 1992), 176-77.

10. "Ebony Interview with the Rev. Jesse Jackson," *Ebony Magazine* (June 1981), 156.

11. "PUSH Celebrates Its 25th Anniversary," *Ebony Magazine* (December 1996), 48.

12. Andrew Billingsley, *Mighty Like a River: The Black Church and Social Reform* (New York: Oxford University Press, 1999), 87-101, 198-206.

13. Ibid., 149-50.

14. Beverly Hall Lawrence, *Reviving the Spirit: A Generation of African Americans Goes Home to Church* (New York: Grove Press, 1996), 177.

15. Bridge Street AME Church Bulletin insert (October 24, 1999).

16. Harvard Divinity School Conference, "A New Urban Agenda: The Black Church's Economic Responsibility" (March 1994), video tape #3.

17. Charles L. Kennedy, quoted in Ernest Holsendolph, "Minding Our Business: Hoping to Serve Churches' Economic Spirit," *Emerge Magazine* (April 1998), 28.

18. Hall Lawrence, *Reviving the Spirit*, 177.

19. See Mark Whitlock, "A New Urban Agenda: The Black Church's Economic Responsibility," Harvard Divinity School conference (1994), video #2: "Models of Church and Community Development." Whitlock is the executive director of First AME Church's Renaissance Program.

20. Tom Robbins, "Gore-Test: Candidate Challenged to Take On Issue of Affordable Housing," *The Village Voice* (July 5-11, 2000). See <http://www.cpn.org>

21. Vida Griffith, quoted in Robbins, "Gore-Test."

22. For information about the CDC, see <http://www.westa.org/cdc.htm>

23. "Church Businesses Spread the Gospel of Self Help," *Ebony Magazine* (February 1987), 61-62, 68.

24. Whitlock, "A New Urban Agenda."

25. Quoted in Susan D. Newman, *With Heart and Hand: The Black Church Working to Save Black Children* (Valley Forge, Pa.: Judson Press, 1994), 25.

26. This organization was developed to bring together the concerns and resources of various black denominations. In addition to allowing the Black Church to better use its collective resources, it also has generated opportunities for cross-denominational conversation and understanding.

27. Alex Poinsett, "Suffer the Little Children: Black Churches Have More Youth-Oriented Programs Than Any Other Institutions," *Ebony Magazine* (August 1988), 144, 146.

28. Ibid., 148.

29. Hall Lawrence, *Reviving the Spirit*, 14.

30. Garth Baker-Fletcher, *Somebodyness: Martin Luther King, Jr., and the Theory of Dignity* (Minneapolis: Fortress Press, 1993), 171-72.

31. Emilie Townes, *Breaking the Fine Rain of Death: African American Health Issues and a Womanist Ethic of Care* (New York: Continuum, 1998), 72.

32. Robert D. Bullard, "Introduction," in *Confronting Environmental Racism: Voices from the Grassroots*, ed. Robert D. Bullard (Boston: South End Press, 1993), 10-11.

33. Charles Lee, "Beyond Toxic Wastes and Race," in Bullard, *Confronting Environmental Racism*, 49; Robert D. Bullard, "Environmental Justice for All," and Karl Grossman, "The People of Color Environmental Summit," in *Unequal Protec-*

tion: Environmental Justice and Communities of Color, ed. Robert D. Bullard (San Francisco: Sierra Club Books, 1994), 3-4, 14-15, and 280 respectively.

34. For additional information on why communities of color have such high concentrations of hazardous industry, and so on, see Regina Austin and Michael Schill, "Black, Brown, Red, and Poisoned," in Bullard, *Unequal Protection.*

35. Harry A. Wheeler, e-mail interview (January 25, 2001).

36. Nancy Wright, A. Cecilia Snyder, and Don Reevers, "Population, Consumption, and Environment," *AME Church Review* (January-March 1995), 32.

37. Karl Grossman, "The People of Color Environmental Summit," in Bullard, *Unequal Protection,* 274-76.

38. Ibid., 274-75.

39. Ibid., 274.

40. James H. Cone, "Whose Earth Is It, Anyway?," in *Risks of Faith: The Emergence of a Black Theology of Liberation, 1968-1998* (Boston: Beacon Press, 1999), 140-41.

41. Cited in N. Jean Sindab, "Introduction," in *National Black Church Environmental and Economic Justice Summit Report* (New York: The National Council of Churches of Christ in the USA, 1993), 3.

42. Ibid.

43. *National Black Church Environmental and Economic Justice Summit Report* (New York: The National Council of Churches of Christ in the USA, 1993), 66-67.

44. See "The Eco-Justice Working Group" at <http://www.webofcreation.org/ncc/Workgrp.html> and <http://www.webofcreation.org/ncc/suggestion.html>

45. <http://www.webofcreation.org/ncc/WGCONG.HTM>

46. <http://www.nrpe.org/mission.html>

47. <http://www.churchworldservice.org/links.html>

48. "Statement of Legislative Principles" at <http://www.pachurches.org/html/values.html>

49. <http://www.thewac.org>

50. Tina B. Krause, comp. and ed., *Faith-Based Environmental Justice Resources for Youth and Children* (Elkhart, Ind.: Environmental Justice Resources, National Council of Churches, 1997).

51. Carol Johnston, *And the Leaves of the Tree Are for the Healing of the Nations: Biblical and Theological Foundations for Eco-Justice* (New York: Office of Environmental Justice, 1997), 2.

52. *101 Ways to Help Save the Earth, With Fifty-two Weeks of Congregational Activities to Save the Earth* (New York: Eco-Justice Working Group of the National Council of Churches, 1990).

5 The Black Church on Health and Sexuality

1. Angela Davis, *Women, Culture and Politics* (New York: Vintage Books, 1990), 55.

2. Emilie M. Townes, *Breaking the Fine Rain of Death: African American Health Issues and a Womanist Ethic of Care* (New York: Continuum, 1998), 39.

3. Edward H. Beardsley, *A History of Neglect: Health Care for Blacks and Mill Workers in the Twentieth-Century South* (Knoxville, Tenn.: The University of Tennessee Press, 1987), 273.

4. Richard C. Schroeder, *The Politics of Drugs: An American Dilemma*, 2d ed. (Washington, D.C.: Congressional Quarterly Press, 1980), 122.

5. Townes, *Breaking the Fine Rain of Death*, 69.

6. Meredith Minkler and Kathleen M. Roe, *Grandmothers as Caregivers: Raising Children of the Crack Cocaine Epidemic* (Newbury Park, Calif.: SAGE Publications, Inc., 1993), 158.

7. U.S. Department of Health and Human Services, *Drug Abuse and Drug Abuse Research—The Third Triennial Report to Congress from the Secretary, Department of Health and Human Services*, DHHS Publication no. (ADM) 91-1704 (Washington, D.C.: U.S. Government Printing Office, 1991), 87, 114.

8. U.S. Department of Health and Human Services, *Third Triennial Report*, 114; Clarence Lusane, *Pipe Dream Blues: Racism and the War on Drugs* (Boston: South End Press, 1991), 50; Davis, *Women, Culture and Politics*, 58-59.

9. Rev. Jesse L. Jackson, "Down with Dope! Up with Hope!" *Ebony Magazine* (August 1988), 134.

10. Ibid.

11. <http://ojjdp.ncjrs.org/action/sec3.htm>

12. "The Church and the Drug Crisis: Ministers Mobilize against 'The Death of a Race,'" *Ebony Magazine* (August 1989), 160-64.

13. <http://www.pachurches.org/html/values.html>

14. Rev. Ronald J. Weatherford, "The Conspiracies that Fuel AIDS," *The Christian Recorder* 149/11 (February 21, 2000), 9.

15. Kenneth S. Robinson, "Touching the Untouchable: A Theological Perspective on AIDS," *AME Church Review* (July-September 1997), 82.

16. Ruby L. Bailey, "Activist Takes AIDS Prevention Advice to Black Churches," *Detroit Free Press* (March 22, 1999). See the *Detroit Free Press* website for details.

17. "For We Struggle: A Call to Action," *The AME Christian Recorder* 150/3 (October 30, 2000), 8.

18. Robinson, "Touching the Untouchable," 86-87.

19. Pennsylvania Council of Churches, "Statement of Legislative Principles" (1999-2000). See <http://www.pachurches.org/html/values.html>

20. <http://www.blackaids.org/kujisource/kuji0300/balm.htm>. The name Balm of Gilead is based on Jeremiah 8:22.

21. <www.balmingilead.org>

22. Randy Boyd, "Balm in Gilead: Just What Does that Mean, Anyway?," at <http://www.blackaids.org/kujisource/kuji0300/balm.htm>

23. "Black Church Week of Prayer for the Healing of AIDS" March 5-11, 2000. See <http://www.balmingilead.org/programs/weekofprayer2001.shtml>

24. Jacob Levenson, "A Time for Healing," *MOJO Wire Magazine* (July/August 2000).

25. Rev. Otis Moss, Jr., quoted in Hilary L. Hurd, "People Watching," *Emerge Magazine* (September 1998), 14.

26. John J. DiIulio, Jr., "Living Faith: The Black Church Outreach Tradition," report 98-3, The Jeremiah Project, the Initiative of the Center for Civic Innovation. See at <http://www.manhattan-institute.org/html/jpr-98-3.htm>

27. "The Church and the Drug Crisis," 161.

28. George D. McKinney, *I Will Build My Church* (St. Louis: Open Door Ministries, 1985), 40-41.

29. Annie Ruth Powell, "From Victim to Survivor: A Journey toward Wholeness," *AME Church Review* (July-September 1997), 29.

30. <http://www.westa.org/counsel.htm>

31. <http://www.aac.org/hivservices_ministry.htm>

32. Cornel West, *Race Matters* (Boston: Beacon Press, 1993), 86.

33. Michael Eric Dyson, *Race Rules: Navigating the Color Line* (New York: Addision-Wesley Publishing Company, 1996), 91.

34. Floyd H. Flake, "Building New Communities," *AME Church Review* (April 1996), 36.

35. Harold M. Rose and Paula D. McClain, *Race, Place, and Risk: Black Homicide in Urban America* (Albany, N.Y.: State University of New York Press, 1990), 103.

36. Fredrick C. Harris, *Something Within: Religion in African-American Political Activism* (New York: Oxford University Press, 1999), 169.

37. Goldie Phillips, quoted in Beverly Hall Lawrence, *Reviving the Spirit: A Generation of African Americans Goes Home to Church* (New York: Grove Press, 1996), 142-43.

38. For a treatment of sexuality in the Black Church, a useful resource is Kelly Brown Douglas, *Sexuality and the Black Church* (Maryknoll, N.Y.: Orbis Books, 1999).

39. Bishop William A. Hilliard, quoted in Thomas B. Romney, "Homophobia in the Black Community," *BlackLight online* 1/4 (November 1979). See at <http://www.blacklightonline.com/phobia.html>

40. Bishop John Hurst Adams, quoted in Juan Carlos Rodriguez, "Struggles of a Black Gay Minister," *Miami New Times* (October 26, 2000). See at <http://www.miaminewtimes.com/issues/2000-10-26/metro2.html>. I am grateful to Jacqueline Trussell for sharing this story with me.

41. "Statement on Homosexuality," *AME Church Review* (October-December 1995), 7.

42. Cornel West, "Christian Love and Heterosexism," in *The Cornel West Reader,* ed. Cornel West (New York: Basic Civitas Books, 1999), 404.

43. Rev. Yvette Flunder, quoted in Rhonda Graham, "And the Choir Sings On," *Sunday News Journal* (Wilmington, Delaware) (October 23, 1994). See at <http://www.qrd.org/www/culture/black/articles/gospel.html>

44. Mindy Thompson Fullilove and Robert E. Fullilove, "Homosexuality and the African American Church: The Paradox of the 'Open Closet,'" *HIV InSite* (February 11, 1998). See at <http://hivinsite.ucsf.edu/InSite-jsp?doc=2098.3803>

45. Michael Eric Dyson, *Race Rules,* 104-5.

46. Elias Farajaje-Jones, "Breaking Silence: Toward an In-the-Life Theology," in *Black Theology: A Documentary History, Volume 2: 1980-1992,* ed. James H. Cone and Gayraud S. Wilmore (Maryknoll, N.Y.: Orbis Books, 1993), 141.

47. Carlton W. Veazey, quoted in Leslie M. Watson, "Breaking the Silence on Sexuality," Seminary Project Focusing on Sexuality Issues in Black Churches (December 21, 2000). I am thankful to Jacqueline Trussell for sharing this story with me.

48. Watson, "Breaking the Silence on Sexuality." Also see <http://www.rcrc.org/current/action.html>

49. For information on the "Keeping It Real" program, see <http://www.rcrc.org/bci/keeping.html>

50. For information on the "Breaking the Silence" program, see <http://www.rcrc.org/bci/breaking.html>

51. Ron Stodghill, II, "God of Our Fathers," *Time Magazine* 150/14 (October 6, 1997).

52. For a brief but informative discussion of this race-relations element, see Michael O. Emerson and Christian Smith, *Divided by Faith: Evangelical Religion and the Problem of Race in America* (New York: Oxford University Press, 2000), chap. 3.

53. James S. Tinney, cited in James H. Cone, *For My People: Black Theology and the Black Church* (Maryknoll, N.Y.: Orbis Books, 1984), 115.

54. Andrea Robinson and Stephen Smith, "Epidemic of Silence: AIDS in the Black Community," *Miami Herald* (May 9, 1999).

6 Sexism and Church Ministry

1. Helen T. Gray, "From Pew to Pulpit: Women's Leadership Roles Challenge Tradition," *AME Church Review* (October-December 1992), 17.

2. Paula Giddings, *When and Where I Enter: The Impact of Black Women on Race and Sex in America* (New York: Bantam Books, 1984), 47.

3. Clarence Taylor, *The Black Churches of Brooklyn* (New York: Columbia University Press, 1994), 169.

4. Cheryl Townsend Gilkes, "'Together and in Harness': Women's Traditions in the Sanctified Church," *SIGNS* 10/4 (1985), 683; and idem, *If It Wasn't for the Women . . . : Black Women's Experience and Womanist Culture in Church and Community* (Maryknoll, N.Y.: Orbis Books, 2000).

5. Ibid., 92-93.

6. Ibid., 95.

7. Gray, "From Pew to Pulpit," 17.

8. Jarena Lee, cited in *Sisters of the Spirit: Three Black Women's Autobiographies of the Nineteenth Century*, ed. William Andrews (Bloomington, Ind.: Indiana University Press, 1986), 29.

9. Ibid., 36.

10. Ibid., 38.

11. Julia A. Foote, "A Brand Plucked from the Fire: An Autobiographical Sketch," in Andrews, *Sisters of the Spirit*, 180.

12. Ibid., 202.

13. Bettye Collier-Thomas, ed., *Daughters of Thunder: Black Women Preachers and Their Sermons 1850-1979* (San Francisco: Jossey-Bass Publishers, 1998), 27-28.

14. Joan Speaks, quoted in Gray, "From Pew to Pulpit," 18.

15. Quoted in Richette Haywood, "A Ministry of Equality and Hope," *Ebony Magazine* (November 1991), 104.

16. Ibid.

17. McKenzie's election in 2000 comes sixteen years after the United Methodist Church elected Leontine T. C. Kelly a bishop. For brief information on this, see

Marilyn Marshall, "First Black Woman Bishop," *Ebony Magazine* (November 1984), 164-70.

18. Jacquelyn Grant, "A Crack, A Break, A Shattering; State of the Glass: A Theological Interpretation of the Election of Bishop Vashti Murphy McKenzie," *The AME Church Review* 116/378 (Summer 2000), 19.

19. Rev. Samuel W. Bacote, quoted in *Daughters of Thunder: Black Women Preachers and Their Sermons, 1850-1979,* ed. Bettye Collier-Thomas (San Francisco: Jossey-Bass Publishers, 1998), 153-54.

20. Ella Eugene Whitfield, "Salvation Is a Discovery Found in Jesus Christ," in Collier-Thomas, *Daughters of Thunder,* 157-58.

21. C. Eric Lincoln and Lawrence Mamiya, *The Black Church in the African American Experience* (Durham, N.C.: Duke University Press, 1990), 44.

22. Rev. Trudie Trimm, quoted in Lynn Norment, "Women Find Success in the Pulpit," *Ebony Magazine* (November 1991), 99.

23. Suzan Johnson Cook, "Religion and Ethics Newsweekly," transcript for show #338 (May 19, 2000). See at <http://www.thirteen.org/religionandethics/transcripts/338.html>

24. Franklyn Richardson, quoted in Gray, "From Pew to Pulpit," 19.

25. Vinson Synan, *The Holiness-Pentecostal Tradition: Charismatic Movements in the Twentieth Century,* rev. ed. (Grand Rapids, Mich.: William B. Eerdmans Publishing Company, 1997), 180.

26. Gilkes, "Together and in Harness," 682.

27. *Official Manual with the Doctrines and Discipline of the Church of God in Christ* (Memphis, Tenn.: Church of God in Christ Publishing House, 1973), 159-60.

28. Cheryl J. Sanders, *Saints in Exile: The Holiness-Pentecostal Experience in African American Religion and Culture* (New York: Oxford University Press, 1996), 137.

29. Jacquelyn Grant, "Black Theology and the Black Women," in *Black Theology: A Documentary History, Volume 1: 1966-1979,* ed. James H. Cone and Gayraud S. Wilmore (Maryknoll, N.Y.: Orbis Books, 1979), 328.

30. Delores Williams, *Sisters in the Wilderness: The Challenge of Womanist God-Talk* (Maryknoll, N.Y.: Orbis Books, 1993), 208.

31. Katie Cannon, "Hitting a Straight Lick with a Crooked Stick: The Womanist Dilemma in the Development of a Black Liberation Ethic," in *Black Theology: A Documentary History, Volume 2:1890-1992,* ed. James H. Cone and Gayraud S. Wilmore (Maryknoll, N.Y.: Orbis Books, 1993), 305.

32. For additional clarification, see Anthony B. Pinn and Anne H. Pinn, *The Fortress Introduction to Black Church History* (Minneapolis: Fortress Press, 2001), chap. 4.

7 Future Considerations

1. Robert Franklin, "Lost Shepherd," *Emerge Magazine* (December-January 1998), 69.

2. Rev. Ernest L. Gordon, "Until We Meet Again: Events of the 46th Session of the General Conference: Reverend Ernest L. Gordon, Turner Graduate," *The AME Christian Recorder* (October 16, 2000), 7.

3. "Church Steps Forward to Close the 'Digital Divide,'" *Christian Recorder* (February 21, 2000), 11.

4. "Net Startup Targets Largest Online Population," *The AME Christian Recorder* (September 4, 2000), 8.

5. Jacqueline Trussell, interview (January 14, 2001).

6. Ibid.

7. Ibid.

8. Richard N. Ostling, "Superchurches and How They Grew," *Time Magazine* (August 5, 1991), 62.

9. Aldore Collier, "A Grand-Slam Homer for Jesus," *Ebony Magazine* (December 1989), 41-42.

10. Rhonda B. Graham, "War: Rev. Fred Price Is Fighting the Church over Racism," *Emerge Magazine* (December-January 1999), 44, 46.

11. Hamil R. Harris, "Growing in Glory," *Emerge Magazine* (April 1997), 51.

12. Ibid., 50.

13. Ibid., 51.

14. Ibid., 52.

15. <http://www.tdjakes.org/ministry_index.html>

16. Quoted in Harris, "Growing in Glory," 52.

Selected Resources

This bibliography provides a sampling of the resources available to those interested in black Christianity as represented by the Black Church. It does not reflect all the materials cited in the notes, and it is not intended to be exhaustive.

Academic Books

History

Du Bois, W. E. B. *The Souls of Black Folk: Authoritative Text, Contexts, Criticism.* Edited by Henry Louis Gates, Jr., and Terri Hume Oliver. New York: W. W. Norton, 1999.

> This ground-breaking book has served to define contemporary understandings of race in America through the concepts of the "color line" and "double consciousness." In addition to a seminal sociological and historical treatment of race relations, Du Bois also discusses the nature of black religion.

Hall Lawrence, Beverly. *Reviving the Spirit: A Generation of African Americans Goes Home to Church.* New York: Grove Press, 1996.

> Hall Lawrence explores the movement of the black middle class back into the Black Church. After a period of absence, most notably during the 1970s and 1980s, "buppies" have made their way back to religious community. According to the author, this results from a sense of disillusionment with material success which fails to fill spiritual needs.

Lincoln, C. Eric, and Lawrence Mamiya. *The Black Church in the African American Experience.* Durham, N.C.: Duke University Press, 1990.

> This book provides an interesting and important discussion of Black Church history and important themes within its development from the 1600s to 1990.

Long, Charles. *Significations: Signs, Symbols, and Images in the Interpretation of Religion.* Philadelphia: Fortress Press, 1986; Aurora, Colo.: Davies Group, 1999.

> Long's book is extremely important for anyone interested in a more theoretically informed discussion of black religion. Using the tools of his training in the history of religions, Long provides a general discussion of religion as it develops as a consequence of contact and conquest in the "new world."

Raboteau, Albert. *Slave Religion: The "Invisible Institution" in the Antebellum South.* New York: Oxford University Press, 1978.

Although published over twenty years ago, this text remains an important introduction to black Christianity during the period of slavery.

Sernett, Milton C. *Bound for the Promised Land: African American Religion and the Great Migration.* Durham, N.C.: Duke University Press, 1997.

The Great Migration represents a major period of religious diversification with black communities; in this respect it is extremely important for any student of black religious history. Sernett's book provides an insightful discussion of the period.

Taylor, Clarence. *The Black Churches of Brooklyn.* New York: Columbia University Press, 1994.

Centered on the development of religious community in Brooklyn, New York, this study explores institutional development as well as the formation of the Black Church's social activism within Brooklyn. The findings presented in terms of Brooklyn are certainly applicable to other communities.

Weisenfeld, Judith, and Richard Newman. *This Far by Faith: Readings in African-American Women's Religious Biography.* New York: Routledge, 1996.

This collection of biographical sketches outlines the involvement of women in the work of the Black Church, including their work in missions, the arts, ministry, and activism.

Wilmore, Gayraud S. *Black Religion and Black Radicalism: An Interpretation of the Religious History of Afro-American People.* Maryknoll, N.Y.: Orbis Books, 1983.

This historical discussion of black religions uses the notion of revolutionary struggle as a lens through which to discuss the development of the Black Church and its central figures. This text is widely cited for its analysis of the "de-radicalization" of the Black Church, through which Wilmore calls attention to the otherworldly nature of the Black Church from the early 1900s to the civil rights movement.

Theology, Ethics, and Biblical Studies

Brown Douglas, Kelly. *Sexuality and the Black Church: A Womanist Perspective.* Maryknoll, N.Y.: Orbis Books, 1999.

At present, this is the only book devoted to this important issues. Through a historical presentation of black sexuality and its construction, Brown Douglas sheds light on the Church's perspective as well as its shortcomings on issues of sexuality.

Cannon, Katie. *Black Womanist Ethics.* Atlanta, Ga.: American Academy of Religion, 1988.

Cannon's book marks one of the early texts in womanist thought. It outlines the moral situation of black women from 1619 to the late twentieth century, using Zora Neale Hurston and other figures to develop a constructive ethic.

Cone, James H. *A Black Theology of Liberation.* 2d edition. Maryknoll, N.Y.: Orbis Books, 1986.

This book is important for students of black religion and religious thought because it represents the first construction of a systematic black theology.

Cone, James H., and Gayraud Wilmore, eds. *Black Theology: A Documentary History.* 2 vols. Maryknoll, N.Y.: Orbis Books, 1992.

For those interested in black theology's history as well as its major figures, themes, and challenges, this two-volume set provides the best concise presentation.

Felder, Cain Hope. *Troubling the Biblical Waters: Race, Class, and Family.* Maryknoll, N.Y.: Orbis Books, 1989.

This volume provides important essays on biblical interpretation within the black American context.

Felder, Cain Hope, ed. *Stony the Road We Trod.* Minneapolis: Fortress Press, 1991.

This volume contains essays covering various dimensions of biblical studies from the perspective of black liberation.

Roberts, J. Deotis. *Liberation and Reconciliation.* Philadelphia: Westminster Press, 1971.

Roberts, one of the early leaders in the black theology movement, counters the movement's strong emphasis on liberation. He argues in this book that both liberation and reconciliation are necessary if the United States is effectively to address racism.

Townes, Emilie. *Breaking the Fine Rain of Death: African American Health Issues and a Womanist Ethic of Care.* New York: Continuum, 1998.

This is one of the few substantive treatments of black religion and issues of health and health care. It provides useful statistics and other relevant information concerning the impact of certain health issues on black Americans. It also provides an important critique of the Black Church's work on issues such as HIV/AIDS.

Williams, Delores S. *Sisters in the Wilderness: The Challenge of Womanist God-Talk.* Maryknoll, N.Y.: Orbis Books, 1993.

This book provides an important discussion of surrogacy as a problematic Christian concept that oppresses black women. Williams argues that surrogacy, understood as theologically connected to the sacrifice of Christ on the cross, encourages black women and other oppressed groups to accept their sufferings as a religious obligation.

Wimbush, Vincent. *African Americans and Biblical Interpretation.* New York: Continuum, 2000.

Drawn from papers given during a massive conference held at Union Theological Seminary, this collection of essays covers various disciplinary perspectives on black Americans and the Bible. It is perhaps the most comprehensive text of its kind.

Black Religious Activism

Baer, Hans A., and Merrill Singer. *African-American Religion in the Twentieth Century*. Knoxville, Tenn.: University of Tennessee Press, 1992.

Putting black churches in the context of other religious communities, Baer and Singer explore the therapeutic and sociopolitical consequences of participation in religious community.

Billingsley, Andrew. *Mighty Like a River: The Black Church and Social Reform*. New York: Oxford University Press, 1999.

Readers will find this book an interesting sociological analysis of the Black Church and its progressive socioeconomic activities. Drawing on local case studies, the author paints a portrait of the Church as social agent. It is similar in many respects to the Lincoln and Mamiya text also listed in this bibliography.

Harris, Frederick C. *Something Within: Religion in African-American Political Activism*. New York: Oxford University Press, 1999.

This book, through an interdisciplinary method, explores the material and nonmaterial resources Christianity has offered the black American struggle for sociopolitical development with respect to issues such as mobilization and electoral transformation.

Paris, Peter. *The Social Teaching of the Black Churches*. Philadelphia: Fortress Press, 1985.

Paris provides an important critique of the Black Church's spotty record with respect to progressive activities geared toward liberation. Whereas Wilmore's text is historical in nature, Paris's work is in the area of ethics.

Sawyer, Mary R. *Black Ecumenism: Implementing the Demands of Justice*. Valley Forge, Pa.: Trinity Press International, 1994.

Sawyer provides an interesting discussion of the Black Church and social activism that cuts across denominational lines.

West, Cornel. *Prophesy Deliverance!* Philadelphia: Westminster Press, 1982.

Few within black theological circles gave much attention to social theory and analysis as part of black liberation theology. This book, the first by West, provides a Marxist social analysis for black theology that argues for black Christianity's prophetic abilities with respect to socioeconomic and political issues in the United States.

Black Church Worship Tradition

Cone, James H. *The Spirituals and the Blues*. Maryknoll, N.Y.: Orbis Books, 1972.

Cone provides a concise theological discussion of the spirituals and the blues as unique forms of black American religious culture.

Costen, Melva Wilson. *African American Christian Worship*. Nashville, Tenn.: Abingdon Press, 1993.

> Costen provides an interesting discussion of the various aspects and aesthetics of worship within the Black Church Tradition.

Harris, Michael W. *The Rise of Gospel Blues: The Music of Thomas Andrew Dorsey in the Urban Church*. New York: Oxford University Press, 1992.

> This book provides an interesting study of gospel music's history and its intersection with various forms of black secular music.

Mitchell, Henry. *Black Preaching: The Recovery of a Powerful Art*. 1970. Reprint. Nashville, Tenn.: Abingdon Press, 1990.

> Mitchell provides a history and thematic study of the black preaching tradition. This is one of the first such studies.

Washington, James Melvin, ed. *Conversations with God: Two Centuries of Prayers by African Americans*. New York: Harper Publishers, 1994.

> The introduction to this volume provides a useful context for understanding the use and significance of prayer in the black American Christian tradition. With the context set, the remainder of the text provides examples of prayer.

Popular Literature

Baldwin, James. *Go Tell It on the Mountain*. New York: The Modern Library, 1995.

> This autobiographical account of Baldwin's life provides a creative depiction of Black Church worship, preaching, and the challenge of salvation under what are often oppressive constraints.

Ellison, Ralph. *Juneteenth: A Novel*. New York: Random House, 1999.

> This novel, edited by John F. Callahan after Ellison's death, is the story of a former preacher turned politician. It gives readers an interesting perspective on Black Church Tradition.

Hurston, Zora Neale. *Jonah's Gourd Vine*. New York: Harper & Row, 1990.

> Hurston's novel deals with the exploits of preacher John Buddy Pearson as he wrestles with the demands of his spiritual quest and the appeal of the physical world.

Johnson, James Weldon. *God's Trombones: Seven Negro Sermons in Verse*. New York: Viking Press, 1969.

> Inspired by energetic sermons Johnson recalled hearing, he wrote this collection of sermons dealing with themes such as creation in the black sermonic style.

Larson, Nella. *Quicksand and Passing*. New Brunswick, N.J.: Rutgers University Press, 1986.

Readers will be interested in the main character's struggle with the Black Church Tradition. It sheds light on the perspective on religion held by many during the Harlem Renaissance.

Thurman, Howard. *Jesus and the Disinherited*. Richmond, Ind.: Friends United Press, 1949.

Thurman, known for his modern mysticism and ability to bridge the gap between various religious communities, applies lessons learned from the life of Jesus to life in the United States.

Walker, Alice. *The Color Purple: A Novel*. New York: Harcourt Brace Jovanovich, 1982.

Written as letters to God and the main character's sister, this book takes the reader into the life of Celie and issues of misogyny, self-identity and worth, and empowerment. In developing a sense of self, Celie begins to wrestle with questions concerning traditional notions of God.

Encyclopedias

Encyclopedia of African and African American Religion. New York: Routledge, 2001.

This anthropologically framed volume provides information on religious culture and institutions as they develop in both Africa and the United States.

Encyclopedia of African-American Civil Rights: From Emancipation to the Present. New York: Greenwood Press, 1992.

This encyclopedia chronicles major events and persons associated with the struggle for liberation within black communities. Although it does not explicitly deal with religion in the manner of the other encyclopedias mentioned here, it provides important context.

Encyclopedia of African American Religions. New York: Garland Publishing, 1993.

Readers interested in biographical information on major figures within the Black Church and other religious organizations will find this volume useful.

Journals and Periodicals

This list includes both academy and church-based publications. For additional church publications readers should contact the various denominations using the Internet information provided below.

AME Church Review

This publication provides articles on topics of general interests to a black church audience, particularly members of the AME Church.

AME Zion Church Quarterly

> This is the major publication for the AME Zion Church. It contains articles related to black religion in general and the workings of the AME Zion Church in particular.

Christian Index

> This is the major publication for the Christian Methodist Episcopal Church. In terms of content, the scope and concerns are similar to those in the *AME Church Review* and the *AME Zion Church Quarterly*.

Journal of the American Academy of Religion

> This is the major outlet for the largest organization of scholars in the study of religion. Readers will find useful reviews of books in black religion as well as articles on relevant topics.

Journal of Black Studies

> As with several of the other journals listed here, the *Journal of Black Studies* is not strictly concerned with the Black Church or religion in general. However, it often contains relevant articles.

Journal of Feminist Studies in Religion

> Although not a journal exclusively concerned with black religious thought, this journal has published some of the most important work in womanist scholarship.

Journal of the Interdenominational Theological Center

> Although recent issues have been dominated by the center's faculty, it is an important resource for materials on the Black Church. And, like the *Journal of Religious Thought*, it often draws a wide range of scholars.

Journal of Religious Thought

> Produced by Howard University, this is arguably the premiere journal strictly devoted to black religious thought.

Theology Today

> Readers interested in articles on black theology and other theological developments related to the Black Church will find this journal useful.

Whole Truth

> This is one of two periodicals published by the Church of God in Christ. The other is *The Voice of Missions*.

The Worker

> This is the missionary and educational quarterly magazine for the Progressive National Baptist Convention. Articles are primarily concerned with the application of the gospel to contemporary social concerns.

Documentaries

"Black Church Video Series on Economic Development." Harvard University—Harvard Divinity School.

> This series of videos, based on a conference co-sponsored by Harvard Divinity School and the Progressive National Baptist Convention, highlights presentations by some of the country's best-known ministers on issues of economic development in black communities. Also recorded are presentations by bank officials and the United States Secretary for Housing and Urban Development. It provides a short but useful introduction to issues of economic empowerment on the level of the local congregation.

"Ethnic Notions." Marlon Riggs.

> In this documentary Riggs provides important information on the development of material and intellectual culture in the United States as they provide rationales for racism. This video puts the Black Church's concern with racist depictions of black Americans in its historical and cultural contexts.

"Eyes on the Prize." PBS Videos.

> This series of eight videos probably represents the most important documentary on the civil rights movement and the Black Church's role in this movement.

"Keeping Faith." Washington Media Associates Production.

> Using Chicago as its primary setting, this documentary discusses the Black Church's role in sociopolitical and economic progress within black communities.

"Religion, Rap, and the Crisis of Black Leadership." Public Affairs Television, Inc.

> In this interview Cornel West discusses religion within the context of black cultural and intellectual life.

"Too Close to Heaven." Films for the Humanities and Sciences. An IBT/CTVC production for Channel 4.

> This documentary presents the history of gospel music as well as its influence on more "secular" forms of musical expression such as jazz and R & B.

Internet Resources

The following is a small sampling of the many resources related to the Black Church and black Christianity in general available on the internet. Every effort has been made to ensure that the URLs are accurate and up to date. However, with the rapid changes that occur in the World Wide Web, it is inevitable that some pages or other resources will have been discontinued or moved, and some content modified or reorganized. The publisher recommends that readers who cannot find the sources or information they seek with the URLs in this book use one of the numerous search engines available on the Internet.

http://www.amecnet.org

> Readers will find this AME Church homepage useful for basic, historical information.

http://www.theamezionchurch.org

> At this site, readers will find basic information concerning the structure and activities of the AMEZ Church.

http://www.blackandchristian.com

> Provides important information on the black church, including articles, as well as links to other sites. It is one of the more useful and comprehensive internet resources.

http://www.churchworldservice.org

> The Church World Service provides assistance to communities suffering from poverty and other forms of oppression. Several of the black denominations participate in its activities.

http://www.cogic.org/main.htm

> This is the official homepage for the Church of God in Christ, with links to other sites of interests to members of the Church of God in Christ.

http://www.c-m-e.org

> This offical CME site provides basic church information as well as links to relevant online conversations.

http://www.cnbc.org

> This is the official website for the Congress of National Black Churches, an institutional partnership between black denominations. The site provides information concerning its various outreach programs.

http://divinity.library.vanderbilt.edu/kmsi/default.htm

> Using this address interested persons can access the Kelly Miller Smith Institute on the African American Church. Readers will find the site's information on conferences and programs interesting.

http://www.gospelweb.org

> This is an interesting site devoted to gospel music.

http://www.morehouse.edu/leadershipcenter/index.htm

> This is the official website for the Leadership Center at Morehouse College. This center houses several initiatives including the Public Influences of African-American Churches project.

http://www.nationalbaptist.org

> This is the offical website for the National Baptist Convention, U.S.A., Inc. It contains useful information on the local, national, and international activities of the convention.

http://www.pnbc.org

> This offical homepage for the Progressive National Baptist Convention includes information on the convention's mission, beliefs and structure.

Index